This is Christianity

This is Christianity

Peter Cotterell

OM
publishing

First published 1985 by InterVarsity Press,
38 De Montfort Street, Leicester LE1 7GP

This revised edition published 1997 by OM Publishing

03 02 01 00 99 98 97   7 6 5 4 3 2 1

OM Publishing is an imprint of Paternoster Publishing
P.O. Box 300, Carlisle, Cumbria, CA3 0QS, U.K.

British Library Cataloguing in Publication Data

A catalogue record for this book is available from the British Library

ISBN 1-85078-252-0

Typset by WestKey Ltd., Falmouth
and printed in the UK by Mackays of Chatham PLC, Kent

CONTENTS

1

Basic Questions

According to David Barrett's *World Christian Encyclopaedia* (Oxford University Press, 1982) Christianity is now found in every one of the 223 countries of the world and some 32.8% of the population of the world claims to be Christian. Although there are something like 20,800 different denominations, all follow Christ, and all call themselves Christians.

> The most fundamental question we can ask about this movement is 'What is Christianity?' This book tries to say, clearly and simply, *This* is Christianity.

1. Why is life so unfair?

The experience is the same for us all: life isn't fair. It would be so nice to be able to say that in life we all get what we deserve. But people cheat and no thunderbolts strike from heaven. People lie and get away with it. In fact a BBC 'Horizon' TV programme ('Liar', 30.10.95) insisted that telling lies is a necessary part of being human and that learning to tell lies is all part of growing up: 'Deception is part and parcel of a wonderful social ability . . . a world without lying wouldn't last very long.' But when a wife lies to her husband about the reason that she will be late home, when a neighbour lies to social security and comes away with a wallet stuffed with illicit cash, when a child is knocked down by a speeding car and the driver lies about his speed . . . we think that they should get their come-uppance. Most often they don't. Some people go right through life lying and cheating and swindling and it never catches up with them. On the contrary, they flourish. Life's not fair. And some people suffer the most appalling injustice.

It was early morning on the ninth of March 1950 in Pentonville Prison, London. In the cold dawn, still protesting his innocence, Timothy Evans was taken from his prison cell and hanged for the murder of his wife and baby daughter. Crucial to the evidence against him was one special witness at the trial, John Christie, who lived in the flat below the Evans family. Three years later that same John Christie was arrested, found guilty of multiple murders and hanged. Ten years further on and the authorities at last admitted their mistake. Timothy Evans had been innocent, just as he had always insisted. The man who had fatally testified against him was in fact the murderer of Timothy Evans's wife and daughter. Timothy Evans was given a free pardon. *Posthumously*. And everything inside every right-thinking person cries out: 'That's not fair!'

And there's the heart-breaking problem of physical suffering which is obviously undeserved. The tiny Siamese twins successfully survived the first operation to separate them, and we all wanted the rest of the process to be successful and for the babes and their parents to live happily ever after. They caught a very rare disease (why them?) and died. The man who scooped a fortune on the national lottery, and a week later was sent to prison for stealing cars . . . why should *he* win, when there are so many people who *deserve* to win?

There's the galling unfairness of overflowing riches and abject poverty. Some while back, in London, a cabinet was being auctioned. Something rather special, I guess, because it went for nine hundred thousand pounds. Nearly a million. The newspapers said the buyer had a bargain, but . . . almost a million pounds for a fancy box? I worked it out at three million meals for hungry people. In a world where people are starving, buying a box for a fortune doesn't seem to make sense. It's not fair.

This cry, 'It's not fair!' is torn out of most of us at some time in our lives. By those experiences of pain, illness, bereavement, accident, hunger, loneliness, war, famine, earthquake. So much suffering, so much pain, and most of the time it seems to be the wrong people who are hurting. We feel instinctively, we cry out from deep inside that life ought to make sense, we demand that it make sense, but still it doesn't.

2. Introducing religion

Religions disagree amongst themselves about almost anything you care to name, but they all agree on this one issue: they all agree that life ought to make sense. Obviously they all agree that it doesn't appear to make sense, but they all agree that it should. Buddhism provides us with the technical term for the fact that life isn't fair. According to Buddhism life is characterized by three things:

- *anicca* – life is impermanent, all is eternally caught up in change.
- *anatta* – life is impersonal, 'you' and 'I' are deceptions, myths, unreal, non-existent.
- *dukkha* – life is unsatisfactory, meaningless, without reason.

Buddhism goes on to explain why life is like this, how we might explain it, and how we then ought to live in such a world. Like Buddhism, all the rest of the world's religions make the same three points:

- life is meaningless, it is characterized by *dukkha* –
- this is *why* it appears to be meaningless, and –
- *this* is how one should live.

Since I shall be saying quite a lot about religion and religions I need to offer some kind of definition of religion. I am aware of scores of definitions of religion, and I expect there are hundreds, if not thousands of definitions. But this is the one I'll be using:

> *Any coherent philosophical system that offers answers to the fundamental questions is a religion*

or, put a little more simply:

> *A religion is any system of thinking that offers answers to the fundamental questions.*

There are three parallel sets of 'fundamental questions':

- Who am I? Where did I come from? Where am I going to? Why?

♦ Who are you? Where did you come from? Where are you going to? Why?

♦ What is this world? Where did it come from? Where is it going to? Why?

All religions offer answers to these fundamental questions. I am not suggesting that we all ask the questions in just the same way, or even that we all put the questions into words. But we still ask them. However stumbling our words may be, however churned up our emotions may be, the time comes when we start asking the fundamental questions.

One advantage of our definition of religion is that it enables us to decide what we mean by a 'religion'. What's more, the definition confirms that what we intuitively recognize as religions are indeed religions (Islam, Hinduism, Buddhism, Judaism, Christianity). The definition also indicates that Marxism is a religion, because it does offer answers to the fundamental questions. For example it answers the first of the fundamental questions, 'Who am I?' by referring to the evolutionary process and responds: 'You are the chance product of the evolutionary process.' But still Marxism does not believe that life is meaningless: there is a law to life, the process of inter-action between any existing system and the present opposition to it, producing a new system. This law may be summarized as *thesis*, *antithesis*, and *synthesis*. This helps to explain why it is that Marxism has usually been in conflict with religions, and particularly in conflict with Christianity. Marxism is itself a religion, and so it has the urge to replace other religions by itself. It has the authoritative answers to the fundamental questions, revealed by Karl Marx, and the answers offered by other religions must necessarily be wrong.

However, the definition excludes Capitalism from the family of religions, because Capitalism does not attempt to answer the fundamental questions.

Having defined 'religion' and stated the fundamental questions, we are in a position to make a very important observation. Careful and honest scholarship shows it is simply not true to suggest that all religions are saying essentially the same thing. John Kane writes:

> Detailed scholarly work in the history of religions has shown . . .
> facile assertions of unity to be without base.
>
> (*Pluralism and Truth*, Scholars Press, 1982, p.17)

The fact is that the world's religions do not disagree merely on unimportant, trivial, secondary matters, but they actually disagree on the essentials. They disagree about the answers to the fundamental questions. Let's look at the answers given by some religions to the three sets of fundamental questions.

3. The three sets of fundamental questions

(i) Who am I? Where did I come from? Where am I going to? Why?

The first set of fundamental questions arises from our own awareness of the nature of life. Life appears to have a beginning and it appears to have an end. It begins with birth and it ends with death. Where was I, if anywhere, before I was born? And where will I be, if anywhere, after I die?

Eastern religions, such as Hinduism and Buddhism open up both ends of the human existence, and reply that you were before you were 'born', and you still will be after you have 'died'. You are caught, trapped, in the endless cycle of existence, *samsara*. Unless something happens to break this cycle you will go on being born, living, dying, only to be born yet again. To some people in the developed world this is a very comforting idea; death is no longer something to fear because it is not, after all, the end. But the majority of those who hold to these views have a more profound understanding of the real world: to be reborn means almost certainly to be dragged back into this awful world of hunger and poverty and disease simply because by far the majority of the world's population live like that. I may be reasonably well off now, but if I return, what kind of life shall I have? Where am I going to?

Buddhism offers *nirvana* as the answer to the 'where?' question. You can escape from the cycle of birth and death by following the 'middle path', the pathway between *hedonism*, the search for pleasure, on the one hand and *asceticism*, the stern denial of all pleasure, on the other hand. And then, when everything that you do is done just *because*, not for pleasure and not for pain, but just *because*, when all desire is snuffed out — then the cycle will end. And the reason is that in Buddhism *desire* is the source of all suffering, and of the samsaric cycle.

Hinduism has a similar goal: the end of the cycle. But Hinduism expects that to be reached by obeying the duty of one's caste, and, perhaps, by one's devotion to god, (this is the so-called *bhakti* or devotional school of Hinduism).

Our problem is that we are trapped in this samsaric cycle by our deeds, by what we did in our previous incarnations.

8

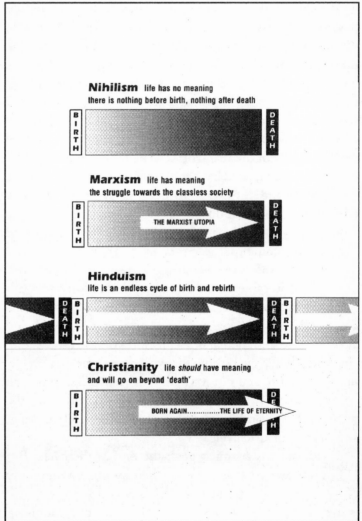

We come into this world already loaded down with our *karma*, the debit balance of the sins committed in the last incarnation, and the one before that, and the one before that. But when that debit balance has been paid off then we can hope for absorption into the Absolute. Either pathway means the end of 'me'. C.S. Lewis made a shrewd comment on the commonly used analogy of a drop of water running into the ocean: if the drop of water runs into the ocean it can be thought of as still existing, but that's the end of it *as a drop*. In other words if I am to be absorbed into the Absolute then that's the end of me as *me* (*Mere Christianity*, p.137).

Christianity responds to this series of questions differently:

> *I am a unique individual. I was created by God. I had a beginning, but I shall not have an ending. Why was I created? In order to come to know my Creator, to know him personally, to enjoy him.*

The answer to the question 'Where am I going?' is complicated by the Christian explanation of *dukkha*, the general unsatisfactoriness of life. Christians agree that life appears to be unsatisfactory. It is so because we have lost that vital relationship with God, the very thing for which we were created. We have become too clever, too self-confident, arrogant. Foolishly we have come to believe that we can manage the affairs of this world without any reference to God. We abuse our power, our knowledge. We exploit the world, God's world, and ruin it. In Africa the Sahel desert spreads. In Europe the seas become polluted, dumping places for our waste. Whole species of animals become endangered, and then extinct. The greenhouse effect means that the earth is getting warmer and the level of the seas is rising. Now scientists admit: it is our fault, not just some inevitable process of the created world. The Christian explanation of *dukkha* is at heart very simple: we have left God out of the equation. Put him back in and all could be very different.

Put God back in and the answer to the question 'Where am I going?' is what it was when humankind was first created: 'To God, to heaven, to paradise.'

But if not? If I will not allow God to put my life straight, forgiving sin past, freeing me from the tyranny of sin present, what then? Then I shall continue to be part of *dukkha*. I shall be discontented myself and I shall make others discontented.

Note, however, the Christian answer: it can never be I, myself, alone, unaided, who by some great effort put myself right. God must do it. I cannot.

So we may ask the question 'Why?' Why did God bother to create *me*? Even more, having created me, and having seen me turn away from him and go my own way, why did he then come seeking me, instead of simply wiping me off his register? If the world's *dukkha* is simply the sum total of all the godlessness of people like me, why doesn't God simply end us all and start over again somewhere in his universe?

The answer is: because of the love of God.

God is not a distant, uncaring, remote, monster. Christianity presents God as a loving Father. He is the loving father that many of us never knew. But he is not merely a sentimental doting grandfather who can be relied on to overlook all the naughtiness of his grandchildren. He is *just*. A *just* God *will* have the books balance: one day either he will settle the debt or you will, but it must be settled.

Years ago I read of a Canadian farmer who decided to challenge the God of Christianity. He hit on the idea of deliberately working on Sunday, the Christian day of rest and worship. After the September harvest he wrote to his local newspaper: 'I ploughed that field on a Sunday, I sowed the grain on a Sunday, I reaped it on a Sunday, and I even sold it on a Sunday. And I made a bigger profit on that field than on any other of my fields.' The editor of the newspaper contented himself with a one-line response: 'God doesn't settle his accounts in September.'

(ii) Who are you? Where did you come from? Where are you going to? Why?

The second series of fundamental questions recognizes that we live in society. There's me and there's you. Surely it's obvious that my understanding of who you are will determine how I treat you. Stalin could exterminate those who opposed him because Marxism believes that 'you' is unimportant. Kolakowski, in *Main Currents of Marxism* (vol.3, pp.81–83) writes, 'Millions were arrested, hundreds of thousands executed.' Again Christianity gives a different answer:

You, too, are a unique individual, and it is not God's intention to lose or to destroy your individuality.

You are not intended to be 'absorbed' into the eternal.

12

That body of yours *is* forever changing: it grows, strengthens, declines, weakens and eventually disintegrates. But *you* are a uniquely created individual, an unrepeatable combination of what you inherited through the genes which came to you from your parents, of what you have learned and experienced in life, and of what God has done for you and in you. You have a unique collection of gifts and abilities, and in that particular combination they are to be found in no one else, only in you. You are irreplaceable and like every other 'one-off' you are priceless. You are valuable, invaluable, to God.

More than that, though. Christianity insists that God has a unique purpose for your life: good, perfect, pleasing (see Romans 12:2). You did not come into existence by accident, the inevitable consequence of a particular sex act of your parents. The sex act has occurred millions of times in history without resulting in conception. When a sex act does result in conception Christians see that as an act of God: God gladly creating new life. It was he who deliberately chose to bring you into being.

For those of us who appear to be nobodies in this world this is a tremendous thought: I am not unwanted. Maybe my parents didn't want me, but God does!

Once more we have a series of very clear answers to the basic questions.

(iii) What is this world? Where did it come from? Where is it going? Why?

Along with Islam and Judaism (but not Hinduism or Buddhism) Christianity teaches that God created the world. It had a beginning and it will one day be put aside, finished with. It is not eternal (as Hinduism suggests), nor is it an illusion (as Buddhism suggests) nor is it a cosmic accident (as Marxism suggests). The earth was uniquely created by God, intended to be 'home' for us. A little further from the sun and it would have been too cold for us, a little closer to the sun and it would have been too hot for us. We have the moon, so that the nights may be lightened, and the earth spins about its axis so that we have night and day. We have oxygen to breathe, an ozone layer to protect us from unacceptable levels of radiation.

But life on Planet Earth is still unsatisfactory. It's easy enough to argue that some of life's catastrophes are man-made, but certainly not all of them are man-made. There's disease, for example – crop failure, pests of all kinds, bacteria. Rabbits are all very well but what about the disease of myxomatosis, that wiped out tens of thousands of them? Where did it come from? If God created the world he surely made a poor job of it?

Not so, replies the Christian. Christians then go on to expand a little on the explanation of *dukkha*, the unsatisfactoriness of life:

♦ This world is not the way it was meant to be.
♦ This world is not the way it is one day going to be.

What is this world? It is a unique home for humanity, created by God.

And where is it going? Well, it appears to be out of control.

Lead us Evolution lead us
Up the future's endless stair;
Chop us, change us, prod us, weed us,
For stagnation is despair;
Groping, guessing, yet progressing,
Lead us nobody knows where.

14

(C.S. Lewis, *Poems*, p.55)

All manner of attempts have been made to put the world back on course again. New political systems: local systems in Africa, international systems such as Marxism – all try to make sense of life, to end the unsatisfactory nature of human existence.

These human systems all seem to start with the assumption that we are each of us basically good, reasonable people, and that we will be prepared to work for the good of others, not merely for our own good. And so, hopefully, we will put the world to rights. But the world doesn't go right, the attempts all end in failure. The reason lies in us. We aren't all reasonable people anxious to work for the good of others. Most of us are selfish, anxious to protect our own rights.

A good many years ago there was a lengthy correspondence in the *Times* newspaper about what is wrong with the world. The series concluded with a typically brief and pithy letter to the editor from G.K. Chesterton:

Dear Sir,
What is wrong with the world?
    I am –
        Yours sincerely,
        G.K. Chesterton.

Ultimately the problems of the world come back to *us*. It's not so much that the *world* is a problem: it's *us*. So this third set of fundamental questions leads us inexorably back to the first set and the second set.

Where is the world going? It appears to be heading into chaos. And is it God's fault? Well, take the unsatisfactoriness of famine. There's no rain and so the crops fail and the people starve. God's fault! Not so! Actually there's more than enough food in the world to feed everyone who is alive today and everyone who is likely to be alive in the foreseeable future. It's *distribution* that's the problem. It's a mad world where Europe actually pays its farmers *not* to grow food, and America stockpiles its grain and beef surpluses, while people in Africa and Asia starve to death every *day*.

But wait! It's too easy to blame America and Europe alone. They are the Third World's favourite whipping boys. In fact we are *all* of us to blame for the mess: black, white, east, west. The Americans wanted to help the starving peoples of Somalia, and in 1994 went into Somalia in an attempt to bring peace to that land so that the food that was available and waiting could be distributed to the hungry. The Somali warlords wanted no interference in their battles: the soldiers did very well, and no-one else really mattered. In neighbouring Ethiopia the Marxist rulers followed exactly the same logic: feed the soldiers and never mind the rest. And some people weren't above taking the powdered milk sent in by Europe and America, and mixing it with chalk powder and then selling the deadly mix on the black market.

Where is this world going? It is heading towards chaos. War, fighting, exploitation, greed, disease, earthquake, famine, all part of the chaos of this world. But the world wasn't created like that:

God saw all that he had made, and it was very good.

(Genesis 1:31)

In Christian teaching it is humanity that is to blame for the chaos. The third chapter of Genesis simply but dramatically records the determination of humanity to go its own way, to leave God out. Simply but powerfully the consequences are spelled out. We become estranged from God and we are doomed to live in a hostile world. In one word, *chaos*.

This chaos is not God's doing, but ours. That's the 'Why?' of the world going into chaos – because of us and our rejection of God, our determination to manage without him. If we knew him, if we cared about what he wants of this world, if we cared about him then we couldn't and we wouldn't do the things that we now find it so easy to do.

4. The cure for chaos

Christianity has both an explanation of the chaos and a cure for it. The explanation of it we have already seen. The cure for it is at two levels, immediate and future.

In the short term, God wants to put a new quality of life, new ambitions, fresh priorities, into us so that we will be able to put God first, others next and ourselves last. In the short term we would then get a better world. To be realistic, we have to admit that it still would not be the best possible world simply because Christianity does not encourage us to believe that large numbers of people will want this new life, will be prepared to live this new way. Christianity is not mere pie-in-the-sky, but the offer of a tough new way, a disciplined way, the way of Christ.

In the longer term, Christianity also has something to offer. There is the expectation that one day the world will display all the order and beauty that it originally had. Paul saw that. Most of the early Christians seem to have been very ordinary people, but Paul was the exception. He wrote a letter to the Christians at Rome and he put the picture very clearly:

> *All of creation waits with eager longing for God to reveal his people. For creation was condemned to lose its purpose, not of its own will, but because God willed it to be so. Yet there was the hope that creation itself would one day be set free from its slavery to decay and would share the glorious freedom of the children of God. For we know that up to the present time all of creation groans with pain, like the pain of childbirth. But it is not just creation alone which groans; we who have the Spirit as the first of God's gifts also groan within ourselves, as we wait for God to make us his children and set our whole being free.*

> (Romans 8:19–23, GNB)

That is the Christian's long-term answer to the unsatisfactory nature of life. God has put me right and can put you right. Between us we can begin to put the world right. One day, however, God will step in decisively to set the whole of creation free, so that we will see God's world as it was always meant to be.

You will have noticed that again and again as we have

looked at the fundamental questions we have come back to ourselves, to people. Yet we need to ask ourselves if we are right in placing humanity at the very centre of our thinking. Is humanity *really* that important?

Well, we are important not because *we* think that we are important, but because God has made us so. But then part of the reason for the general unsatisfactoriness of life is that we make ourselves important, but without any reference to God. A simple question and answer from the Westminster Shorter Catechism, a sort of official quiz book on the Christian faith, puts the Christian view neatly:

- ◆ 'What is the chief end of man?'
- ◆ 'Man's chief end is to glorify God, and to enjoy him for ever.'

Life ought not to be about personal success and personal fame, fun and fortune. It ought to be all about God, who should be the centre of our lives. What we think, say, do, should all be controlled by this thought: God created me so that I might glorify him and enjoy him for ever.

Christianity insists that life will make sense only when it is related to God. The logic of this idea is very straightforward. If my life and yours must be summed up, assessed, between the two terminuses of birth and death then it will never make sense. Life is meaningless. Life simply is not fair. But once I allow God to enter into the account new hope comes flooding in. One of those terminuses isn't a terminus at all; just a change station. Now it becomes possible to make sense of life. The whole of life, here, between birth and 'death', and then after death, in glory – it can all make sense. The whole of creation can make sense.

Humanism recognizes the unfairness of life and simply says: 'Life isn't fair. It's sad, but that's the way it is. You just have to accept it.' Buddhism says: 'Life isn't fair, but that's because you don't recognize it for what it is, one big illusion, *maya*. The suffering is illusion. The world is illusion. Other people are an illusion.'

Christians respond: 'Life isn't fair, but open your eyes, look to God. You are not a mere cosmic accident, you are not an illusion, but you are unique, the unique creation of God. He made you so that you might glorify him and enjoy him for ever. Get right with God! Then you will be changed and your little part of the world will be changed. One day it will all be changed, but God wants to start *now*.'

> We haven't said much about Jesus so far. Before we can look in any detail at just how God changes us we have to look at Jesus, because he is the one who actually makes the change possible.

2

Jesus – The Answer

We have seen that the world's religions can be regarded as a collection of attempts to supply answers to the fundamental questions: 'Who am I?' 'Where did I come from?' 'Where am I going to?' 'Why?' and so on. For example, as Gautama the Buddha pondered human existence he was struck particularly by the fact of universal suffering. He sensed that suffering came from desire, the desire for things, the desire for power, even the natural desire to be. He suggested that we could eliminate suffering if we could stop *wanting* things. If desire causes suffering then by ending desire we will end suffering. But how could we end desire? He suggested what is sometimes called the noble eight-fold path, a 'middle way' between the search for happiness, or *hedonism*, and self-denial, or *asceticism*. It means neither laughing too much, nor crying too much, but walking calmly and quietly through life. Buddhist tradition refers to the fig tree, under which Gautama sat while he puzzled all this through, as the tree of enlightenment.

Karl Marx chose rather a different place for his thinking: the Library of the British Museum, in London. But he was tackling the same problem: the apparent meaninglessness of life, suffering, oppression, inequality. His explanation was different. According to him the suffering was mostly due to the human class system and the inevitable enmity between the classes. Eliminate the classes and you would eliminate the suffering: there would be enough for all.

For Christianity the answers to the basic questions come to us not from our own thinking, and not even from our search for God. They come from God himself, from the way in which he has revealed himself, firstly in the Bible and then, and very especially, in Jesus.

The name 'Jesus' is itself significant because of its meaning: 'The Lord saves' (see Matthew 1:21). The name presupposes a situation from which people need to be saved, and indicates that God has someone who can save them.

Jesus was also known as 'The Christ'. This word is the Greek equivalent of the Hebrew 'Messiah', and both words mean 'anointed'. In Hebrew culture a person was anointed with oil as a sign that he was being called to some special task. Kings were anointed, and so were priests and – sometimes – prophets. In the case of Jesus it would seem that his work included all three: he was prophet, priest and king.

Jesus was, of course, a great teacher. But when he offered his teaching to the Jews they noticed something very different about it. He assumed that he possessed some special authority. The other Jewish teachers, or rabbis, taught only what they had learned from another rabbi and they were careful to quote the other rabbi. Jesus didn't. He simply said 'I tell you . . .' The change was remarkable, and Jesus claimed that it was because he had come from God.

Gautama the Buddha had thought about life and had come up with an explanation. Marx went to his library books and came up with an explanation. Muhammad went outside Mecca to a cave on Mount Hira, and came back to Mecca with an explanation. But Jesus claimed to have brought the explanation with him. From God. And that wasn't all: he claimed that in some sense he actually *was* God, God incarnate.

1. The Jesus story: his birth

The life story of Jesus has an unusual beginning and an out-of-the-ordinary conclusion. But then if he was God we would expect that. The unusual beginning first: Jesus had a human mother but no human father. The unique story of the life of Jesus on earth starts with a unique event of conception: Jesus was born of a mother who was a virgin.

The story is told simply in Luke's gospel. The angel Gabriel is sent to Mary to tell her that she is to give birth to a son whom she is to name 'Jesus'. He will be known as the Son of the Most High God. Not surprisingly Mary is perplexed and responds: *I am a virgin. How, then, can this be?* (Luke 1:34).

It's worth noting that Muhammad knew of this account of the birth of Jesus, and he recorded Mary's words to Gabriel as 'How can I have a son when no mortal has touched me?' (Qur'an, Sura 19 v.20). In fact the Qur'an makes reference to the virgin birth of Christ again in Sura 3, and all Muslims believe that Jesus was born of Mary who was a virgin.

In the Bible account the evangelist Matthew explains this miracle as the fulfilment of a prophecy made long before by Isaiah (see Matthew 1:22–23 and Isaiah 7:1–16). At the time

King Pekah's Israel

the prophecy was given, the Israelite kingdom was divided.
Pekah was king of the northern part, Ahaz was king of the
southern part. Pekah joined up with Rezin, king of Syria,
and the two attacked Ahaz. Jerusalem was besieged. Isaiah
prophesied, however, that the two kings would soon give
up the siege and return to their own countries. And Isaiah

gave the people of Jerusalem a sign to assure them of the truth of what he was saying:

> *The Lord himself will give you a sign: a young woman who is pregnant will have a son and will name him 'Immanuel'. By the time he is old enough to make his own decisions, people will be drinking milk and eating honey. Even before that time comes the lands of those two kings who terrify you will be deserted.*

(Isaiah 7:14–16, Good News Bible)

Like a good many other prophecies in the Bible, this prophecy had two points of fulfilment: one near the time when the prophecy was made and second, hundreds of years later. The first fulfilment came in Isaiah's own lifetime, somewhere around 730 BC. Jerusalem was besieged, a young woman had a baby, and before that baby could grow up and start to make any decisions of its own the besieging armies were gone.

But Isaiah had used two very interesting words in his prophecy, one referring to the mother and one referring to the child. The word he used for the mother could simply mean a young woman, but it could also mean a virgin. In those days morality was very strictly observed and a young woman would be a virgin. So there are two points of fulfilment of the prophecy and two meanings of the word. In Isaiah's day it was not a virgin who conceived and had a child, but a young woman. Matthew, however, took the second meaning of the word, and he therefore used the Greek word *parthenos* which means 'virgin'.

Now for the second word Isaiah used: he said that the child would be called 'Immanuel', which means 'God with us'. When Semitic people like the Jews name their children they often use a name which is a comment on some event connected with the baby's birth. I remember a baby being named 'Late Harvest' because he was born when his parents were rather old. In the case of Isaiah's prophecy the name 'Immanuel' was given to the baby because of the miraculous deliverance of Jerusalem from the siege of the two kings. In fact the two kings heard of political unrest in their own countries and went back to deal with it. So the name 'Immanuel', 'God with us', fitted the situation. God was on their side.

25

The full significance of the name, however, is seen in the second fulfilment, when Jesus was born. Jesus was more than a prophet, more than a sign. He was 'God with us', he was God coming amongst us. He was not here as a sign that God would deliver humankind from the Roman armies or from World War One, but that he would deliver us from our ongoing battle with ourselves, with our own human nature, our fallen nature, sin.

This prelude to the account of the life of Jesus is very important. It marks a unique beginning, prophesied seven hundred years earlier. This shows God stepping into the world he had created, not as some kind of superman, not as a king, but as a miraculously conceived baby: God with us.

Clearly this view of the birth of Jesus is very different from that of people who see Jesus simply as a man. They may see him as a particularly good man, they may see him as a remarkable teacher, they may even see him as a prophet to the Jewish people, but still just as a man, interpreting, explaining the world as he found it, as he saw it, as he understood it. By contrast, the Bible presents a *unique* man. For us our existence begins when we are conceived. But not for Jesus. Jesus steps into the world from beyond it, from eternity. This is what Christians call the *incarnation*. It is God becoming man, God stepping into the world, God not summoned into the world by some human sex act, but being born of a virgin. God leaving eternity and embracing time. God with us, God like us in every way except that in all his life Jesus did no wrong. It was a unique beginning to a unique life.

2. The childhood of Jesus

Jesus was born into a poor family. Mary, his mother, eventually married Joseph, a carpenter, they lived in Nazareth, and it seems that later they had several children. The gospel writer Mark refers to Jesus' mother and brothers and sisters (Mark 3:31–32). We know very little about his childhood. Probably he went with the family to Jerusalem each year for the Passover celebrations. Certainly we know that when he was twelve years old he astonished the teachers of the Jewish law in Jerusalem by some of the questions he asked them; and by some of the answers he gave to *their* questions (Luke 2:46–47).

It is interesting to note the way in which, during that visit to Jerusalem, Jesus gently corrected a slip of the tongue by Mary. When the party from Nazareth set off for home again, Jesus was left behind. Mary and Joseph then had to go back to the city to find him.

When eventually they found him, Mary was very upset and said to him:

> 'Son, why have you treated us like this? Your father and I have been anxiously searching for you.'
>
> 'Why were you searching for me?' he asked. 'Didn't you know I had to be in my Father's house?'

(Luke 2:49)

Mary said '. . . your father and I . . . '
Jesus said '. . . *my Father's house.*'

3. Growing up

It's likely that Jesus spent some part of his childhood looking after the few sheep and goats that even poor families owned. And he probably also spent long hours watching Joseph at work, making stools, beds, axe- handles, and yokes, for the necks of the oxen that did the ploughing. Perhaps this was the background to his gentle invitation given years later:

> Come to me, all you who are weary and burdened, and I will give you rest. Take my yoke upon you and learn from me, for I am gentle and humble in heart, and you will find rest for your souls. For my yoke is easy and my burden is light.

(Matthew 11:28–30)

4. His ministry: Jesus as preacher

At about the age of thirty Jesus chose a small group of twelve followers, and began some three years of almost incessant travel over the five thousand or so square miles of Herod's kingdom. As he went he taught and he healed.

The Jewish teacher, or 'rabbi', was not merely a lecturer. He expected his students to absorb his total lifestyle and to learn his teaching by heart. Jesus seems to have followed their example. The twelve followers of Jesus were expected to leave their jobs as fishermen or whatever, to follow the Rabbi.

Yet Jesus was different from other rabbis. He was, and his followers knew that he was, both teacher and Lord. He once said to them: *You call me 'Teacher' and 'Lord', and rightly so, for that is what I am* (John 13:13). It was not just his own followers who recognized that he was different from the usual run of rabbis; the ordinary people recognized the difference, too. As we have already noticed, the rabbis did not claim any authority for themselves, but always quoted other rabbis from the past as their authority. Jesus didn't:

> *When Jesus had finished saying these things, the crowds were amazed at his teaching because he taught as one who had authority, and not as their teachers of the law.*
>
> (Matthew 7:28–29)

5. Jesus and the Kingdom of God

One of the great themes of Jesus' teaching was *God's Kingdom*. Right at the beginning of his gospel, Mark says that Jesus

> . . . *went into Galilee, proclaiming the good news of God. 'The time has come,' he said. 'The kingdom of God is near. Repent and believe the good news!'*
>
> (Mark 1:14–15)

This remarkable theme is a reminder to us that the world is *not* out of control. God rules over it. But this rule of God does not mean that we have no freedom. We are not like clockwork machines, wound up by God and doomed to carry on our amusing tricks until the clockwork runs down. We are free, free even to do things that are contrary to the will of the King.

Our situation is rather like living in a country where the government knows about every case of law-breaking. No one can so much as exceed the speed limit without the authorities knowing. So efficient is the government that every law-breaker is known, is caught and is punished. If such a country existed the people would still be free to break the law, but they would know that if they chose the way of crime then they would have to take the consequences.

Of course this is an imperfect analogy. But it's not a bad analogy. It's not unlike the situation assumed by Jesus' preaching of the Kingdom of God. And that picture is very different from the picture of the world that is painted by, say, Hinduism. In Hinduism my present condition is determined not by me but by my *karma*, my fate, the inescapable 'balance-carried-forward' from my previous life and all the previous lives before that. And that debit balance is added to by the daily debit balances I accumulate in this life, so that tomorrow is already determined by today and by all my yesterdays.

The picture is also different from the picture painted by Islam, where the rule of God is taken to be absolute. History is already written down in the 'Preserved Tablet' in heaven. I cannot depart from that history because it includes *my* history. The most commonly heard phrase in all Arabic is the phrase *inshâ' Allâh*, 'If God wills'. The most famous and important and largest of the Muslim schools of theology, the Ash'arite, denies human freedom and teaches an all-embracing determinism.

When Jesus spoke of the Kingdom of God it was to invite people to recognize God's rule and to submit themselves to it, not because of the privileges that would then be theirs, but simply in recognition that he is God. The Jewish people had misunderstood God's message to them: they had thought that because God gave them the Law and sent to them the prophets that this gave them special privileges, as though God cared for them and for no one else. Eventually national pride led to national disaster. Instead of being free they became part − a small and insignificant part − of the vast and powerful Roman empire.

Of course there were always hopes that they might be free again. Rebellion? Revolt? Would some great leader come to set them free? A new Moses to lead them out of captivity?

A new David to be their king? Jesus reminded them of what they had long forgotten in their preoccupation with politics: he reminded them of God and the kingdom of God.

6. Seven parables about the Kingdom of God

Matthew 13 contains seven parables Jesus told about the Kingdom of God. A parable is a story that explains an idea that might otherwise be difficult to understand. These seven parables illustrate what Jesus had to say about the kingdom of God.

(i) The parable of the man sowing seed

Naturally the results of sowing seed depend on the kind of ground that the seed falls into: soft, rich, prepared soil, weed-infested ground, ground trampled hard by people constantly walking over it, rocky ground. And there's the first thing that Jesus has to say about me and the Kingdom of God. If I am hard, bitter, filled with pride, self-sufficient, selfish, crude and rude, then even if the good seed comes to me, even if I hear about the Kingdom of God, I won't want it, the seed won't take root, no plant will grow.

(ii) The parable of the farmer who planted good seed and his enemy who planted weeds in the same field

Obviously, when the good seed sprouted and the weeds also began to grow there was no way that his labourers could pull up the weeds without also damaging the main crop.

Here is an illustration that might help those people who say that they won't come into the church because of the mixture of people they see already in it. True, there are some nice people. But there are also some people who are definitely not nice: carping, critical (and hypocritical), proud, affected, self-righteous, and even cheats and liars and the immoral. True enough, they are all to be found in the church. And like the weeds in the field they might all of them claim to be part of the main crop. The parable warns us that God doesn't expect his labourers to weed the fields ourselves, now: we'd probably get the wrong ones out. No, the real crop will become apparent at harvest time, when what grows in the field will be harvested and then separated out into two lots, one for the barn and one for the fire.

Don't judge the church too harshly by what you see when you stand outside looking in. After all, you could be in there yourself one day . . .

(iii) The parables of treasure hidden in a field, and of a merchant looking for pearls

32

There really was treasure hidden in a field, and the one way of being sure of getting the treasure was to buy the field: never mind the cost. The merchant was ready to pay anything to buy a really fine pearl. No price would be too much.

The pearl is the kingdom. The question is how much is it worth to us? It's true that in reality we can't buy our way into the kingdom, and the parable doesn't suggest that we can, but the parable does make it clear that there is a price to be paid for getting into the kingdom. It may be the price of being misunderstood: people around may well label you a religious fanatic; all this talk about God is so strange! What's more – and oddly enough – our honesty may well offend people, make them feel uncomfortable, especially if they are not all that honest themselves. A truly honest person is a rebuke to everyone around, and so the honest person may well lose friends.

In some parts of the world the result of entering the kingdom may be much more serious: it may mean the loss of a job, being disowned by the family, even death.

This parable is telling us that there may well be a price to be paid for entering the kingdom: but it's worth the price to gain that pearl.

(iv) The parable of the fishermen and their catch

No doubt Jesus' listeners had frequently seen the fishermen of Galilee coming ashore with their nets filled with fish of all kinds. They would then sit on the shore and sort out the good from the bad, the eatable from the inedible, throwing the useless ones back into the sea again.

Said Jesus: that's how it will be at the end of the age, when the king comes to take up his kingdom. It will be a time for sorting things out. The good is kept, the bad is thrown out, the good into the kingdom, and the bad . . . well, *not* into the kingdom.

Built into this parable is a warning: there really is a kingdom to be won. And there really is the possibility of being shut out of the kingdom. To put it bluntly, there is a heaven to win and a hell to shun.

(v) The parables of the mustard seed and of the yeast

The tiny mustard seed grows into quite a bush, big enough for birds to nest in. The yeast, worked into the dough, exerts its raising power right through the dough.

So the Kingdom of God had small beginnings: maybe Jesus had in mind that little group of totally unimportant individuals who were his disciples. But before sneering at the small beginnings it might be as well to consider the end, the consequences, the results of the small beginnings. Not just the world-wide church, but the return of the King and the bringing in of the Kingdom of God. It is true that throughout the centuries most of the people of the kingdom have been rather ordinary people. But God seems to have delighted in picking out a fisherman like Peter or a shoe-mender like

William Carey or a young do-gooder like Jackie Pullenger and using them to build his kingdom. Sent out into all the world . . . and the world is changed because of them.

34

> Jesus' emphasis on the Kingdom of God helps to explain some of the answers that Christians give to the fundamental questions of chapter one. Where did I come from? Where did you come from? Where did this world come from? God made us and God made it. The world for us to live in and us to live in his kingdom. Where are we all going to? If we are with the King then we are going to his kingdom. For us this present world may appear to be out of control, we have to admit that our king is not ruling, his will is not being done, but the day is coming when it *will* be done. And if we are not with the king, then where are *we* going? The answer to that is: we are *not* going into his kingdom.

7. Jesus and miracles

The gospels describe how Jesus cured people who were ill, brought dead people back to life, changed water into wine at a wedding, walked on the surface of the Sea of Galilee, commanded a storm to cease, and fed a vast crowd with just a few loaves of bread and some fish. The Qur'an states quite simply that Jesus was able to heal the sick, raise the dead and cure those suffering from leprosy (Sura 3 verse 43).

The stories are told simply and without apology. Each miracle is performed in response to some particular need, never merely to prove that Jesus was capable of performing miracles or to impress people so that they would join his followers. The assumption of the writers seems to be: 'This is Jesus. He did these marvellous things. But of course: he is God with us.'

Miracles are: significant – amazing – inexplicable – demonstrations of authority.

They are *amazing* because they are *inexplicable*. There is nothing in ordinary life with which we could compare them. So, for example, when Jesus cured a man who was paralyzed, just by a single sentence – '*Rise, take up your bed, and go home*' – the response of the crowd who saw the miracle of healing actually happen is understandable:

> *Everyone was amazed and gave praise to God. They were filled with awe and said, 'We have seen remarkable things today'.*

> (Luke 5:26)

The miracles of Jesus were *significant*: they weren't mere conjuring tricks. In the miracle referred to above, of the healing of the man who was paralysed, Jesus used the occasion to talk about sin and how *it* might be cured. Having given a vivid illustration of his power over physical illness, he suggested that if he could do *that* particular impossible act, which could be checked out immediately by anyone wishing to do so, then it was not unreasonable that he could also do the other apparently impossible act, forgive sin.

Of course the miracles did not prove that Jesus was God incarnate, God with us. Other people in both Old and New Testament times performed miracles. Elijah, Elisha, Peter, Paul, all brought dead people back to life (1 Kings 17:17–23, 2 Kings 4: 8–37, Acts 9:32–42 and Acts 20:7–12). But if they didn't prove that Jesus was God with us they were still very significant. John commented after Jesus had turned water into wine at the wedding in Cana:

He thus revealed his glory. and his disciples put their faith in him.

(John 2:11)

No matter who performs them, miracles are always demonstrations of *power*. *Someone's* power. This aspect of miracle is particularly important in relation to Jesus' miracles of exorcizing demons. These acts of power clearly relate to a theme we have already touched on: the reality of two kingdoms, the Kingdom of God, and a Second Kingdom, a Satanic kingdom. There is an evil power which is opposed to the power of the Kingdom of God. In some sense we are all of us in the one kingdom or the other, and the Second Kingdom is as real as the First. We do not know precisely what 'demons' are (certainly not those comic figures wearing red tights and carrying pitchforks) but they are presented in the New Testament as spiritual beings which act on behalf of the Satan, much as those other spiritual beings the angels act on behalf of the Kingdom of God. And angels are not to be pictured as white night–dress–clad male figures equipped with wings and clutching harps rather than pitchforks, but as God's messengers (which is what the name 'angel' means in Greek). The action of Jesus in exorcizing demons demonstrates the supreme power of *his* kingdom over the Second Kingdom.

Incidentally, although Islam does not teach the existence of a Satanic *kingdom*, it does teach the reality of *Shaitan* (= the Hebrew 'Satan') or *Iblis* (= the Greek *diabolos*) and of the *djinn*, spiritual beings, some of whom are disobedient to God.

In Matthew 12 Jesus deals with a man who is both blind

and dumb. In this particular case Jesus diagnoses the disease as being due to demonic influence. It is noticeable that Jesus never suggested that *all* diseases had their origin in the demonic, but that *some* did. He healed this man, so that he could see and could speak. The Pharisees, who themselves believed in the reality of the demonic, claimed that Jesus used demonic power to exorcize demons. But as Jesus at once pointed out, '*If Satan casts out Satan he is divided against himself; how then can his kingdom stand?*' The significance of the miracle lay in the power it demonstrated:

> *If it is by the Spirit of God that I cast out demons, then the kingdom of God has come upon you . . . .How can one enter a strong man's house and plunder his goods, unless he first binds the strong man?*
>
> (Matthew 12:28–29)

When he was in the town of Nazareth Jesus was confronted in the synagogue by a man who was tormented by an evil spirit. Jesus ordered that spirit out: 'And when the demon had thrown him down in the midst, he came out of him . . .' (v.35). Once again we are told how the crowd reacted: 'What is this word? For with authority and power he commands the unclean spirits, and they come out' (v.36).

Perhaps it is understandable that people in the western world today find it difficult to believe either in the Second Kingdom and the Satan, or in miracles. As C.S. Lewis has suggested (*The Screwtape Letters*, ch.7), we can't believe in the figure in red tights and so we refuse to believe in the real figure hiding behind it.

The objections to miracles seem to take three forms:

- ♦ I've never seen a miracle, and I can't believe what I've never seen.
- ♦ Miracles are simply perfectly ordinary events exaggerated.
- ♦ Miracles cannot happen.

38   The first argument actually gains in strength if I can go on to say that none of my friends has ever seen a miracle either. However this can be a dangerous route to take because if we do expand the number of our friends too rapidly we are rather likely to come across people who think that they *have* seen a miracle. Although I have not personally seen a miracle, two of my friends claim that they have. One was a cancer that simply disappeared, the other a baffling illness that put my friend off work for weeks, but which was simply dismissed, instantaneously, by the prayer of a friend who went to visit him. If I were not a Christian and if I did not believe in miracles I could say that I had never seen one, but I would certainly have to modify any statement I might care to make regarding the opinions of my friends. I might, of course, modify my statement by saying that neither I nor my friends have ever seen a *real* miracle, but that would merely involve a redefinition of 'miracle' allowing me to decide what was and what was not, a *real* miracle. And since I do not believe in miracles I would inevitably never find one.

In fact inexplicable healings in response to prayer have occurred with some regularity throughout history. The theologian Philip Melanchthon was brought back from the very edge of death through the prayers of Martin Luther, who wrote to his wife on 2 July 1540:

Philip was verily dead, and, like Lazarus, has been raised from the dead. God, the dear Father, hears our prayers. This we can understand, although we often do not believe it.

John Wesley, in the eighteenth century, was involved in a rather odd healing incident. He was on his way to a preaching appointment when his horse went lame. Wesley recorded in his diary that he dismounted, laid his hands on the horse and prayed for healing. The lameness went.

This argument – 'I have never seen a miracle and so I do not believe that miracles happen' – is weak. After all, there are so many things that we have not seen and yet believe in: viruses and quarks and kangaroos and the Sahara desert and the space probe Galileo. The fact is that although I may not have seen these things I won't really have to look very far amongst my friends before finding someone who says 'Well, I have!' And that is exactly what we would expect with miracles: they are unusual events. Not many people have seen one, but some people say they have.

The best attested modern miracle is the miracle at Fatima in Portugal, and this took place with some seventy thousand witnesses. Three children, Lucia, Francisco and Jacinta, claimed to have seen the Virgin Mary, who promised that a miracle would occur in Fatima on 13 October 1917. An enormous crowd gathered: some to see the miracle, some to note that the promised miracle did not occur. Among these last were the journalists, and especially Almeida, the editor of a secular anti-cleric newspaper, O Seculo. They all saw the same thing: the sun danced, whirled, spiralled, and continued to do so for nearly ten minutes. As it appeared to spiral closer and closer to the earth so the people began to panic; and then the sun returned to its normal place. The phenomenon was visible twenty miles away, although nothing unusual was recorded by Lisbon Observatory. Almeida, still a sceptic, nonetheless confirmed the inexplicable event. It seems very different from the biblical miracles: it seems to have no particular point to it, but certainly it was what any reasonable person would call a miracle.

The second argument is that so-called miracles are no more than natural events that have been exaggerated. It has been suggested that Jesus did not walk on the surface of the sea of Galilee: his disciples only saw him in the early morning mist, when he was simply splashing through the shallows of the seashore. Because of the howling wind and the flying spray and the tiredness that inevitably followed a long night, and because they later wished that they might have seen Jesus walking on the sea the fishermen in the boat added a bit here and a bit there to their story until they had quite forgotten what they *had* seen.

Similarly, what 'really' happened when five thousand people are supposed to have been fed with just five small loaves of bread and two fish, the packed lunch of a little boy, was that when the boy gladly offered his dinner to Jesus everyone else was so ashamed that they pulled out the packed lunches that they all carried (and had been concealing for fear that they might have to share it!) with the result that everyone was fed.

I think it's fair to say that the *only* information we have about these two events, Jesus walking on the water, and the feeding of five thousand, is to be found in the Bible. There is no ambiguity about either story: the writer intended his readers to understand that Jesus walked on the water and that he miraculously produced enough food to feed five thousand people *and* have twelve baskets of fragments left over (see Mark 6:30–44 and 45–53). Now it is entirely open to people to say 'I don't believe it.' But if we decide to reject these stories then we must beware of a certain danger:

41

> What we may not do is to invent something to put in the place of what we reject. There is an analogy here with those sceptics who find that they cannot believe the biblical account of the trial, death and resurrection of Jesus and undertake to tell us 'what actually happened'; Caiaphas was really trying to save Jesus. It was all really part of a Zealot plot, Joseph of Arimathaea actually took Jesus down alive from the cross [incidentally the Ahmaddi sect of Islam reintroduced this idea at the beginning of this century; other Muslims simply deny that Jesus was crucified at all], etc. There is no harm in such conceits as long as they are recognized for what they are, sheer fiction. But anyone who takes them seriously is more credulous than the most naive believer in the biblical text.
>
> (G.B. Caird, *The Language and Imagery of the Bible*, p.60)

Believe the stories or else don't believe them, but it is simply dishonest to insist that they *don't* say what every honest reader knows they *do* say.

The third argument against miracles, if it can be called an argument, is the flat assertion that miracles *cannot* happen. People cannot walk on water, and so they have not done so. To walk on water would be contrary to the laws of physics. Suns don't dance, such behaviour would not merely be contrary to the laws of physics but would quite literally rock the universe.

We have observed the universe carefully over centuries

now, and we know pretty well how the universe works. Experiment confirms the laws we have formulated from our observations. To which the Christian might reply: 'But your 'laws' are no more than deductions from your observations. Surely if I observe someone walking on water or the sun dancing, then you as a scientist have somehow to take my observations into your laws?' And I would want to add that some of the most important discoveries about our universe have been made precisely because some scientist somewhere has observed something contrary to existing laws and has been bold enough to insist on the new something being included in new laws. The discovery of radioactive decay by the Curies is just one example, and of the complexity of planetary motion by Kepler is another. It is unscientific to exclude some observations from our theories simply because they make things too complicated or, even worse, simply because we don't believe in them.

For the fact is that our universe is not the nice tidy law-regulated thing we sometimes imagine it to be. Physicists know only too well that once we start to probe the fundamentals of the universe all the tidy understandable and comfortable laws seem to dissolve and turn into questions of probability. I may know where the *laboratory* is, but I can never be sure of where that *electron* is: probably *here*, but there is also a calculable possibility of it being *there*, or even *there*.

Actually it is worthwhile pausing here to draw attention to the recent important changes that have occurred in our thinking about the universe. Before the seventeenth century the world appeared to most people as somewhat chaotic – 'in which witches and demons, angels and 'Acts of God might intervene at any moment'. This world was replaced by

> an ordered sequence of cause and effect. By the end of the nineteenth century that picture had become universal . . . .The laws of science were as the law of the Medes and Persians which altereth not; an absolute rigidity conditioned man's whole nature, physical, mental and moral. In such a world there was no room for freedom, responsibility or standards of good and evil . . . .
>
> (Professor C.E. Raven, in an address to the 1953 Convention of the Institute of Physics, published in the *Bulletin* of the Institute, July 1953)

43

It is not difficult to see how it is that in a survey taken amongst British teenagers in 1995 the majority confessed that they did not know right from wrong: the first generation since Christianity came to Britain that has faced that moral vacuum.

There has been a third stage in the development of scientific thinking about the universe. In place of abstract rules formulated about things (and people were no more than things), Einstein showed us a world characterized by the concept of *relativity*. Everything is to be interpreted in terms of the *observer*. Lengths, masses and velocities, which had been regarded for centuries as absolutes, all turned out to be in some way relative to us, to those who observed and measured them.

Einstein was followed by others. Heisenberg introduced his *principle of indeterminacy*, that because we cannot say anything of any event unless we observe it, and because our observation of the event will always interfere with the event, we can never know what the event itself actually was. We can use ordinary light to view an ordinary event, but to view the sub-microscopic events occurring amongst atoms we need a different kind of radiation. The smaller the wavelength of the radiation, the more accurately we can observe sub-nuclear events. *But* the smaller the wavelength, the more powerfully does the radiation influence the event! Put very simply: if you know *where* it is you don't know *what* it is, and if you know *what* it is then you don't know *where* it is. As Professor Raven said in the same lecture:

> The recognition that there is a constant but unpredictable element of variability in the whole order of nature transforms the cast-iron sequence of the old concept into a process in which change and creativity can and do occur. The difference between the two . . . may be quantitatively minute: it is philosophically immense.

So the Christian might respond to the person who will not believe in miracles: 'A little more humility is called for on your part. You refer to the laws of physics: where did they come from? You refer with confidence to what can and cannot happen in this universe: do we yet know what is and what is not possible? Supposing that God *is*. Supposing that it was *he* who started it all, and that *he* created a world of order and placed there both the macroscopic, the large-scale rules by which we normally order our lives, and the microscopic and infinitely more complex laws that govern the nuclear and sub-nuclear world with all its uncertainties? What then?

'You say that you have never seen a miracle. There are many things that you have not seen and yet in which you believe. And maybe there are some things that we cannot expect to see without faith – not a "blind" faith that will believe anything, but an educated faith that finds the life and the teaching of Christ taking us along the way, which alone enables us to take the final step which links time to eternity.'

45

The Jesus story began with a miracle: his birth from a virgin. It reached its climax in another miracle, the resurrection. In between those two miracles are others, and all of them are signs, shouting to us: 'Stop! Look! Think! Who is this Man?'

> To enable us to answer *that* question we turn next to the crux of Christianity. Not the life and the teaching of Jesus, but his death and resurrection.

3

Winner or Loser?

In a house in Calcutta a Hindu placed around the walls of one room key phrases from the world's religions. From Buddhism there was the mystical 'Hail to the jewel in the lotus.' From Islam was the invocation that stands at the beginning of each chapter of the Qur'an, 'In the name of God, the merciful, the compassionate.' From Confucianism there was the aphorism, 'The sage relies on actionless activity.' Hinduism was represented by 'Tat tuam ati' – 'That thou art!'

There was one biblical text, found in both Old and New Testaments, and apparently perceived as somehow lying at the heart of the Christian faith. The words were spoken by Christ from the cross:

> My God, my God, why have you forsaken me?

Probably every Christian would recognize the insight of the Hindu who chose those words to represent Christianity. Here, in words spoken by Jesus from the cross and from the very edge of death, is the key to the understanding of Christianity. Wherever Christians are free to gather together and to share in Holy Communion, taking bread and wine as Jesus did with his followers before his death, there they consider, meditate on the mystery of those words, 'My God, my God, why have you forsaken me?'

It is significant that each one of the writers of the four gospels places the emphasis not on the life of Jesus, not on his teaching, not even on his miracles, but on the last few days of his time on earth. John, for example, actually devotes nearly half of his gospel to the last week of Jesus' life, and nearly 20 per cent of it to an account of his trial, death and resurrection.

1. The facts

The basic facts of those last days are quite clear. For some three years or so Jesus travelled about Galilee, up in the north of Israel, and Judea, down in the south, preaching, teaching and healing. Throughout this time there was a growing hostility to him from the religious leaders of the Jews: the Scribes, who were the lawyers of the day; the Pharisees, who prided themselves on the strictness of their religious practices; the Sadducees, who were particularly angered by Jesus' talk of resurrection.

Then, as now, there was one great annual celebration for the Jews, more important than all the other religious festivals: Passover. In Jerusalem, just before the Passover celebrations, somewhere around the year AD 32, Jesus was arrested by the Jewish authorities and accused of blasphemy. They handed him over to the Roman authorities, but since the Romans would scarcely be interested in a charge of blasphemy, he was charged now with sedition – accused of 'speaking against Caesar'. The Roman procurator, Pilate, sentenced him to death. He was taken outside the city and crucified. After hanging on the cross for six hours he died.

Because of the approaching Jewish holy day, the Sabbath, his body was removed from the cross and hurriedly placed in a nearby rock tomb. There was no time for the customary anointing of the body with the appropriate oils and spices and ointments. His followers had to be content with carefully noting the location of the tomb so that they would be able to return as soon as the Sabbath was over, to carry out the anointing.

The tomb was closed in the traditional way, by a large stone rolled across the entrance. The Jewish authorities knew Jesus had promised his disciples that he would die and be buried, but on the third day he would be alive again, and so they placed a guard over the tomb to ensure that no one was able to interfere with the body.

Despite these precautions, when some of the women who were among his followers arrived at the tomb at daybreak on the Sunday morning to anoint the body of Jesus, the tomb was empty.

Then, for some forty days, in an entirely unpredictable way, Jesus was seen, alive, by various people. Paul gives an impressive list of them in 1 Corinthians 15:3–8. So far as we know he appeared only to believers. Finally, after forty days, these appearances abruptly ceased. Some of his followers actually saw him as he was 'taken away' from them:

> . . . *he was taken up before their very eyes,*
> *and a cloud hid him from their sight.*

(Acts 1:9)

2. The case against Jesus

Jesus was born in Bethlehem in southern Palestine. Wise men from the east, possibly from Persia (now Iran), had seen some sign telling them of the birth of a king of the Jews. They came to Jerusalem seeking him. Herod listened to their story and was at once fearful of the possibility of a rival king, one who would have more right to the throne than he had, being only half-Jewish. He sent soldiers to kill all the male children in Bethlehem under the age of two years. But he was too late: already Joseph and Mary, with the baby, had escaped to Egypt. From there they were eventually able to return safely to Nazareth, further north in Galilee, where Jesus grew up.

The history of the Jewish people was remarkable because of the regular appearance of prophets, messengers chosen by God, men who spoke out for God, and who not infrequently spoke out concerning future events. There had been Elijah and Elisha. There was Isaiah, and his contemporary, Hosea. Malachi was the last of these prophets. After Malachi there was an ominous silence, a break in the line of prophets lasting for more than four hundred years. The voice of one more prophet then broke the silence. His name was John, soon to be known as John the Baptist, John-the-Baptizer. He proclaimed the imminent coming of the promised Messiah:

After me will come one more powerful than I, the thongs of whose sandals I am not worthy to stoop down and untie. I baptize you with water, but he will baptize you with the Holy Spirit.

(Mark 1:7–8)

John had identified himself with an ancient prophecy. He was, he said,

> *A voice of one calling in the desert,*
> *'Prepare the way for the Lord, make straight paths for him.'*
> (Matthew 3:3, which refers back to Isaiah 40:3)

John was the voice. Jesus was the promised Lord.

People were quick to grasp and to accept John's message. Someone was at hand, someone who would deliver them, perhaps even deliver them from their Roman conquerors. In the past God had sent them such deliverers, men and women. Were they now about to see the coming of the long-promised anointed king, the Messiah, sent by God to deliver his people?

In chapter two we saw that Jesus was described as the 'Christ' (Greek), or the 'Messiah' (Hebrew), both words meaning 'Anointed'. We also saw that kings were anointed, and so were prophets, and so were priests. If Jesus was, in fact, the Christ, the Messiah, was he the anointed King, the anointed prophet or the anointed priest?

(i) Jesus: the promised Messiah

In the Old Testament the history of God's people is shown to be directed through a succession of warrior figures, sent by God, freeing the people from one tyranny after another. Israel was in fact a tiny, insignificant nation surrounded by political giants. She existed as a separate nation only by the grace of God. But there was a downside to that. Israel simply assumed that God would get them out of every difficulty and that they had no corresponding duty to God. Then they had to be reminded that their relationship to God was two-way: loyalty and faith on their side, grace and protection on his. Consequently their history was a long succession of freedom, independence, comparative peace, and then pride, followed by defeat and oppression, discouragement, weakness, and then repentance. Now came the deliverer, a warrior figure to deliver them from their disgrace, people such as those whose exploits are recorded in the Book of Judges – like Othniel, and Ehud, the woman Deborah, Gideon.

In the prophecy of Daniel we find a solitary reference to an unnamed future Messiah-deliverer. Daniel wrote of seventy 'weeks' at the end of which time there would be an end to sin and iniquity would be atoned for. A most holy place would be anointed, and there would be 'an anointed prince' who was to be 'cut off', after which the end would come. This series of prophecies (as we have seen, like many other prophecies) had two points of fulfilment, the first in the time of the Maccabees, when Judas, nicknamed 'Maccabaeus' (= 'the Hammer'), delivered the nation from Antiochus Epiphanes, who was doing his best to stamp out the worship of Yahweh, and the second in Jesus the Messiah. The prophecy itself produced amongst the Jewish people, and especially amongst the people of Galilee, an expectation that a messiah would come, someone as powerful as Judas Maccabaeus had been.

(ii) A Suffering Messiah

But there was a second strand of prophetic teaching in the Old Testament, focusing on a suffering Messiah, a 'Servant of the Lord'. This theme is developed principally in the Book of Isaiah.

This contains four passages which are often called the Servant Songs: 42:1–4; 49:1–6; 50:4–9 and 52:13–53:12 (actually there are other references in Isaiah to this servant, seventeen in all, from Isaiah 41:8 to Isaiah 53:12). The fourth song, especially, pictures not a conquering Messiah, like Judas Maccabaeus, but a Suffering Servant.

Who was this Suffering Servant? This is how Professor G.B. Caird answers the question:

> Was the servant to be the whole nation or only a remnant, to be many, few or one? The reason why modern scholars have endlessly debated these questions is that the prophet himself did not know the answers. It is as though he had published an advertisement, 'Wanted, a servant of the Lord', accompanied by a job description. He was undoubtedly aware that many famous men, such as Moses and Jeremiah, had sat for the composite portrait he was drawing. What he could not know was that in the end there would be only one applicant for the post.
>
> (*The Language and Imagery of the Bible*, p. 58)

The Suffering Servant was to be Jesus.

So there were two strands of teaching running through the Old Testament, each promising a deliverer, but one strand promising a King-Messiah and the second offering a Suffering Servant. The Jewish people of Jesus' day grasped at the possibility that he might be the promised King-Messiah. Jesus himself gave them no encouragement in this mistaken idea. In fact he repeatedly warned his followers against it, urging them to play down this identification of himself as King-Messiah. While it was right in principle they had misunderstood its application. He was, indeed, God's deliverer, but not in the political sense that both his own immediate followers and the mass of the people expected. In fact his own followers were still thinking of a political kingdom even after his death and resurrection. They asked him: 'Lord, are you at this time going to restore the kingdom to Israel?' (Acts 1:6)

Well, he wasn't. Not at that time. He had come with a different purpose.

Yet during those years of travelling around Palestine it was impossible for Jesus to conceal his unique powers. He healed people of all kinds of illnesses, and who could prevent those who were healed from talking about it? He gave sight to the blind, and even people suffering from leprosy were healed. Three times he raised the dead. The Qur'an, incidentally, refers to these demonstrations of his power (in Sura 5:109–110), although it does not describe any particular miracle. Although he appears to have regularly told the people he healed not to talk about their experiences, inevitably they talked. Even King Herod heard about what he was doing (Mark 6:14). Not surprisingly, Jesus came to be seen by the religious leaders as a challenge to their authority. Their lives could not match the simplicity and purity of his. Their words lacked the authority his teaching had. Worse still, he could not only talk, but he could also perform acts of mercy and power which they could not duplicate. Politics and religion were never far from each other in Palestine, and the politicians, too, saw Jesus as a threat to themselves, and to political stability.

Jesus had consistently refused this political role for himself.

We see this in the account of the feeding of the five thousand, recorded in all four gospels. Those who were present on that occasion could not doubt that a miracle had happened, and inevitably asked a crucial question about Jesus: if he had brought about this miracle, then who and what was he? It was equally inevitable that their thoughts would go to the King-Messiah. A well-known prophecy in Deuteronomy 18:15–19 predicted that one day another prophet like Moses would appear. When Israel was in the desert after escaping from slavery in Egypt, Moses had miraculously fed his followers with food from heaven, the 'manna'. It was natural to conclude that Jesus was the promised prophet-like-Moses: 'Surely this is the prophet who is to come into the world', they said (John 6:14). Their immediate determination was to proclaim Jesus king. His reaction was significant.

> *Jesus, knowing that they intended to come and make him king by force, withdrew again into the hills by himself.*
>
> (John 6:15)

Jesus' mission was not there to become embroiled in politics. He had not come as King-Messiah but as Servant-Messiah. He had come to challenge the kingdom of Satan, not the kingdom of Herod.

3. The trial of Jesus

Jesus was never sentenced by a Jewish court. The religious leaders intended that Jesus should be executed, and only the Roman authorities could pass the death sentence. If his case could be passed on to the Romans for trial then on the one hand the outcome could very well be his execution, and on the other hand responsibility for his death could conveniently be placed on the Romans.

An informal interrogation by the Jewish leaders did take place:

> The chief priests and the whole Sanhedrin were looking for evidence against Jesus so that they could put him to death, but they did not find any. Many testified falsely against him, but their statements did not agree.
>
> (Mark 14:55–56)

Eventually they wearied of this unsatisfactory approach, and so they asked him outright: '*Are you the Christ, the Son of the Blessed One?*' (Mark 14:61)

The question was an important one. For one thing, it faced Jesus with the question of whether he was, or was not, the Messiah, the Christ. For another, the priest who asked the question had used the strongest possible form of address in putting this question; as Matthew 26:63 renders it, 'I charge you under oath by the living God.' Thirdly, the question was important because it gave to Jesus the opportunity of making clear to these sophisticated Jewish theologians exactly who he was and what he meant by that word 'Messiah'.

Jesus had to reply and he did:

> I am . . . and you will see the Son of Man sitting at the right hand of the Mighty One and coming on the clouds of heaven.
>
> (Mark 14:62)

This is obviously an important piece of evidence for us as we try to understand who Jesus was. And of course it was important to the Jews who were interrogating him. The answer first of all confirms that Jesus was claiming to be the Messiah. But it is very significant that he then went on to explain what the term 'Messiah' meant by referring not to the miracles he had performed, not to his teaching, not even to his miraculous birth, but to the Old Testament, to a psalm

56 of David and to a prophecy from Daniel.

The Lord says to my Lord: 'Sit at my right hand, till I make your enemies your footstool'

(Psalm 110:1)

In my vision at night I looked, and there before me was one like a son of man, coming with the clouds of heaven. He approached the Ancient of Days and was led into his presence. He was given authority, glory and sovereign power; all peoples, nations and men of every language worshipped him. His dominion is an everlasting dominion that will not pass away, and his kingdom is one that will never be destroyed.

(Daniel 7:13–14)

By referring to the psalm and to this prophecy Jesus was making it clear that he was not merely 'one of them'. He was different: his entire ministry was the fulfilment of prophecy and whatever might happen at this trial these men would one day see him vindicated, coming in triumph to God, seated in power. But there was still more than that to it. The prophecy refers to one who was given authority, and, very significantly, glory, and sovereign power, and as if that were not enough the prophecy actually pictures the whole world worshipping him. The mere reference to two scriptures represented a complete confession that he was, indeed, the Messiah, and an explanation of what that meant.

The explanation given here is not merely a twentieth-century attempt to read Christian significance into a first-century story. Those Jews who heard Jesus at once understood the implication of what he had said. The High Priest himself expressed what they all felt:

> '*Why do we need any more witnesses?* . . . . *You have heard the blasphemy. What do you think?*'

57

> (Mark 14:63–64)

We note the nature of the charge: blasphemy. It would not have been blasphemy if Jesus had contented himself with claiming merely to be another prophet, someone like John-the-Baptizer, for example. He would not even have been guilty of blasphemy had he claimed to be Messiah: the Jews did not expect the Messiah to be a divine figure, but a human figure. And notice that Jesus did not use the forbidden word 'God' in his answer, but 'Mighty One', so he was not being accused of blasphemy because he had pronounced the Name of God. He was accused of blasphemy because he claimed divinity. He claimed to be God. He claimed that he would be worshipped.

The response was unanimous: they all recognized that what Jesus had said was blasphemous because in their view it could not possibly be true. They all agreed that Jesus should die. And they agreed to hand him over to the Romans for formal trial and execution.

Of course the Romans could not be expected to be very interested in the religious arguments of their Jewish subjects. Indeed, when the Jews first took Jesus to Pilate his reply (John 18:31) was entirely predictable: 'Take him yourselves and judge him by your own law.'

Here was the problem that kept on reappearing in the formal trial before Pilate. If Jesus was being charged with blasphemy there was evidence enough to condemn him, but blasphemy was not a matter that would give concern to the Romans. On the other hand, if the Jewish leaders changed their approach and accused Jesus of sedition that certainly would concern Pilate. But there appeared to be no evidence of sedition: Pilate's verdict (Luke 23:4) was, 'I find no crime in this man.'

Ultimately a thinly-veiled threat from the Jewish leaders secured the death sentence they wanted:

> 'If you let this man go, you are no friend of Caesar. Anyone who claims to be a king opposes Caesar.' When Pilate heard this, he brought Jesus out and sat down on the judge's seat at a place known as The Stone Pavement.
>
> (John 19:12–13)

It was now that Pilate sentenced Jesus to death. If Caesar were to hear that a man claiming to be King of the Jews had been arrested, accused, tried and then released, the judge at that trial would have a good deal of explaining to do at his own inevitable subsequent trial at Rome. Pilate dared not take that chance. Jesus must die.

4. Jesus on the cross

Jesus was arrested on what Christians now remember as Maundy Thursday, the evening of the Last Supper. He was crucified on what we call Good Friday. And he came back from death on what we call Easter Sunday.

The Qur'an does not accept these historical facts. This

is what it says in Sura 4 verses 157–8. (The translation is that of Mohammed Marmaduke Pickthall, an Englishman who became a Muslim and translated the Qur'an into English. Most Muslims accept his translation as correct.)

> And because of their [the Jews] saying: We slew the Messiah Jesus, son of Mary, Allah's messenger. They slew him not nor crucified, but it appeared so unto them; and lo! those who disagree concerning it are in doubt thereof' they have no knowledge thereof save pursuit of a conjecture; they slew him not for certain, but Allah took him up unto Himself.

According to Islam Jesus was not crucified. Most Muslims believe that before Jesus was arrested he was taken up by Allah into the third heaven. Allah then made Judas look exactly like Jesus, so that Judas was arrested and crucified, not Jesus. Many Muslims will point to a book called The Gospel of Barnabas and insist that this alone is the true gospel, and that it sets out the arrest and crucifixion story as the Qur'an has it, but in much more detail. There are six important things to be said about this Gospel of Barnabas.

- ♦ First – the 'Gospel' has nothing to do with the Apostle Barnabas, who is mentioned in the book of Acts.
- ♦ Second – it has no connection with the early Christian Greek Epistle of Barnabas (which dates from the middle of the second century and was not written by the apostle).
- ♦ Third – it was most probably written in Italian in the sixteenth century by a disaffected Franciscan monk, Father Marino.
- ♦ Fourth – although we know of Italian and Spanish

versions there has never been any evidence of a Greek or Hebrew or even an Arabic version.

♦ Fifth – it contradicts both the Qur'an (for example it says that Mary gave birth to Jesus without pain, where the Qur'an specifically refers to her pains) and also the New Testament (oddly placing Nazareth by the Sea of Galilee).

♦ Sixth – there is no question of Christians having tried to conceal the existence of this work, as some Muslim writers have claimed. It was translated into English by Lonsdale and Laura Ragg and published by the Oxford University Press as long ago as 1907.

They crucified Jesus at nine o'clock in the morning. From the cross Jesus spoke seven times. First he asked God's forgiveness for those who crucified him. Then he made provision for his mother, Mary: John was to take care of her. He promised one of the two men who were crucified with him that on that same day he would be with Jesus in Paradise. He cried, '*I thirst!*' Finally he triumphantly declared, 'It is finished', before using words from the evening prayer used by Jewish children: '*Father, into your hands I commit my spirit.*'

But central to the whole of the crucifixion, the key to any understanding of it, are the words with which we began this chapter, the sentence singled out by that Hindu in Calcutta, '*My God, my God, why have you forsaken me?*' We know very few of the words actually spoken by Jesus. The gospels are written in Greek, but Jesus spoke in Aramaic, a dialect of Hebrew. So when the gospels record something said by Jesus it is a Greek rendering of Jesus' Aramaic words.

But here (Mark 15:34) are the actual Aramaic words spoken by Jesus: '*Eloi, Eloi, lama sabachthani*', '*My-God, my-God, for-why you-have-forsaken-me?*'

The seven words from the cross

61

The central saying is recorded by Matthew and by Mark, using the precise Aramaic words that Jesus used: **'Eloi, Eloi, lama sabachthani?'**

'*Father, forgive them, for they do not know what they are doing*' LUKE 23:34

'*Dear woman, here is your son*' '*Here is your mother*' JOHN 19:26-27

'*I tell you the truth, today you will be with me in paradise*' LUKE 23:43

'Eloi, Eloi, lama sabachthani?'
MATTHEW 27:46
'My God, my God, why have you forsaken me?'
MARK 15:34

'*I am thirsty*' JOHN 19:28

'*It is finished*' JOHN 19:30

'*Father, into your hands I commit my spirit*'
LUKE 23:46

5. The cross and Psalm 22

'*My God, my God, why have you forsaken me?*' – these are the opening words of Psalm 22. Although written about one thousand years before Christ's crucifixion the psalm provides a remarkable commentary on that crucifixion: indeed it might almost have been written for the occasion.

The Jewish understanding of Psalm 22 is that it refers to the collective sufferings of the entire Jewish people, and their eventual deliverance. But Jewish commentators have also applied the psalm to David's sufferings, possibly when Saul was hunting him. Certainly the psalm must have had some immediate application when it was first written: someone or some particular event must have been in the mind of the writer.

Christians see the psalm as prophetic, looking forward to the sufferings of the Messiah-Jesus.

The psalm falls into two parts:

♦ The theme of verses 1–21 is the undeserved suffering of the speaker.
♦ The contrasting theme of verses 22–31 is praise for his deliverance.

If this were a piece of music we would say that in the middle there is a change of key, from the minor to the major. In fact the psalm remarkably runs parallel with the experience of Jesus at the cross, from his suffering to his death and then to his resurrection.

Psalm 22:1-24

MY GOD, my God, why have you forsaken me?
  Why are you so far from saving me,
  so far from the words of my groaning?
O my God, I cry out by day,
  but you do not answer,
  by night, and am not silent.

Yet you are enthroned as the Holy One;
  you are the praise of Israel.
In you our fathers put their trust;
  they trusted you and you delivered them.
They cried to you and were saved;
  in you they trusted and were not disappointed.

But I am a worm and not a man,
  scorned by men and despised by the people.
All who see me mock me;
  they hurl insults, shaking their heads:
"He trusts in the LORD; let the LORD rescue him.
  Let him deliver him, since he delights in him."

Yet you brought me out of the womb;
  you made me trust in you even at my mother's breast.
From birth I was cast upon you;
  from my mother's womb you have been my God.
Do not be far from me,
  for trouble is near and there is no-one to help.

Many bulls surround me;
  strong bulls of Bashan encircle me.
Roaring lions tearing their prey
  open their mouths wide against me.

64

I am poured out like water,
  and all my bones are out of joint.
My heart has turned to wax;
  it has melted away within me.
My strength is dried up like a potsherd,
  and my tongue sticks to the roof of my mouth;
  you lay me in the dust of death.
Dogs have surrounded me;
  a band of evil men has encircled me,
  they have pierced my hands and my feet.
I can count all my bones;
  people stare and gloat over me.
They divide my garments among them
  and cast lots for my clothing.

But you, O LORD, be not far off;
  O my Strength, come quickly to help me.
Deliver my life from the sword,
  my precious life from the power of the dogs.
Rescue me from the mouth of the lions;
  save me from the horns of the wild oxen.

I will declare your name to my brothers;
  in the congregation I will praise you.
You who fear the LORD, praise him!
  All you descendents of Jacob, honour him!
    Revere him, all you descendents of Israel!
For he has not despised or disdained
  the suffering of the afflicted one;
  he has not hidden his face from him
  but has listened to his cry for help.

4

Resurrection

His followers were *not* expecting it. On Sunday some of them went to the rock tomb where his body had been hastily placed on the Friday evening, the traditional anointing of his body begun by Nicodemus incomplete. The tomb was open; the body was gone.

1. Witnesses to the resurrection: Mary of Magdala

Jesus was crucified at nine o'clock on that Friday morning, died at three o'clock that same afternoon, and when Pilate had assured himself that he was dead permission was given for the body to be removed from the cross and for Jesus to be buried. Saturday, the Jewish holy day of sabbath rest from work, began at six o'clock that evening, and so the burial was necessarily hurried, completed just before the sabbath began.

Very early on the Sunday morning a group of women including Mary Magdalene went to the tomb. The great stone that had been rolled across the entrance to the tomb was rolled back: the tomb gaped open, and it was empty. Now began a long series of extraordinary appearances of Jesus to his followers.

The very first, to Mary Magdalene, took place right there at the tomb, very soon after the women had made their momentous discovery of the empty tomb. The other women went to tell the men of what had happened, leaving Mary at the tomb. Soon Peter and John arrived and they went into the tomb. What they found was not a scene of disorder, as it would have been if grave robbers had broken in. The neatly folded burial clothes were like a silent message: 'These are no longer needed.'

John and Peter left, but Mary Magdalene remained, standing there, outside the tomb, weeping, simply not understanding what had happened, nor what had become of the body of Jesus. Mary had a particular reason for her devotion to Jesus. According to Luke (Luke 8:2) he had cured her of a desperate illness. It seems possible that she had a wealthy background since she and others like her provided Jesus and his followers with a certain amount of financial help. She had been one of the small group noted by John as being at the cross. Matthew says she was there at the tomb when the body of Jesus was placed there by Joseph of Arimathea. And here she is again, hoping to find . . . not Jesus, but his body. She peered into the dimness of the tomb only to be further confused by the sight of two seated angelic figures. She turned away – it was not angels she wanted but the body of Jesus!

Then Jesus himself came to her. Dazzled by the contrast between the obscurity of the tomb and the glare of the sunlight, blinded by her tears, she didn't recognize the man who stood there. Perhaps he was the garden attendant? (The Greek word is not used anywhere else in the New Testament and the translation 'gardener' is a little misleading: the garden where Jesus had been so hastily buried would certainly have an attendant, a 'keeper'.) Perhaps he had moved the body? He spoke first:

> *'Woman, why are you crying? Who is it you are looking for?'*
> *'Sir, if you have carried him away, tell me where you have put him and I will get him.'*
> *'Mary?'*
> *'Master!'*

(John 20:15–16)

67

2. Witnesses to the resurrection: Thomas

Mary Magdalene was not the only one of Jesus' followers to find it hard to believe in his resurrection. Thomas was another, although he was one of the original group of twelve, the 'apostles', chosen by Jesus himself. Even the apostles weren't expecting the resurrection! Jesus actually appeared to them on the evening of the first Sunday in an upstairs room in Jerusalem. But for some reason Thomas wasn't there, and when the rest of them told him that they had seen Jesus, alive, Thomas refused to believe them:

> *Unless I see the nail marks in his hands, and put my fingers where the nails were, and put my hand into his side, I will not believe it.*

(John 20:25)

Thomas was emphatic. Maybe he was still stunned by the crucifixion of Jesus. Maybe he knew how ready we are to delude ourselves with false hopes. Maybe he had heard what Mary and the other women claimed to have found at the tomb. Had he heard Mary herself talking about her encounter with Jesus – was he simply writing off the women as too emotional to be trusted, and the other ten apostles as ready to swallow any wild yarn? In the original language he didn't just say 'I will not believe it'; his words were much stronger, a double negative: 'I'll never believe it', 'I can't possibly believe it.'

A week went by. Once again the apostles were together, and this time Thomas was with them. Once again Jesus appeared amongst them. After giving the usual Jewish greeting, '*Peace be with you*', he turned to Thomas, and made it quite clear that although he had not been visibly present when Thomas had expressed his unbelief he had been there, he knew:

> *Put your finger here; see my hands. Reach out your hand and put it into my side. Stop doubting and believe.*

(John 20:27)

It seems clear from John's account that Thomas didn't need to put his fingers into those scars, nor to feel the wound in Jesus' side, made after his death by the spear of a Roman soldier. Thomas's surrender was immediate:

> *My Lord and my God!*

Some people have written off this account of Thomas and his doubts as sheer fiction. They have argued that the idea of the criminal being nailed to a cross is absurd, because nails would either not have been strong enough to support a human body, or if they had been strong enough, they would simply have torn their way through the hands and feet. Jesus, they say, would have been tied to the cross. But the toughness of the nails used for crucifixion was proverbial. In addition, the ankle bones of a man in his early twenties named Jehohanan, crucified in the first century, were found in 1970 by Jewish archaeologists, excavating on the Mount of Olives, with the nail which passed through both ankles and a piece of his cross *still in place*. Thirdly, although ropes *were* used in Egypt to bind victims to their crosses this was looked on as a peculiar Egyptian idea.

This confession by Thomas, *My Lord and my God*, is amazing, a total surrender to Jesus. Abandoning his doubts, he acknowledged Jesus not merely as his Master, but as God: 'My *Kyrios*, Lord, my *Theos*, God.'

But perhaps that was just his temperament? He could have been making a terrible mistake, even a blasphemous one, when he spoke of and to Jesus in such a way? He had been wildly wrong previously, when he refused to believe that Jesus had appeared to the other apostles; maybe this was an equally wild mistake, but in the opposite direction?

Jesus himself settled the matter once for all :

> *Because you have seen me you have believed; blessed are those who have not seen and yet have believed.*

> (John 20:29)

Jesus didn't correct Thomas. On the contrary he identified his confession as an act of faith: '. . . *you have believed.*' Contrast what Jesus says here, to Thomas, with what an angel said to John in that amazing last book of the Bible called Revelation. There John, dazed with all the wonders he has seen, thrilled with all that he has been told, falls down to worship the angel, God's messenger:

> *I fell down to worship at the feet of the angel . . . but he said to me 'Do not do it! I am a fellow servant with you and with your brothers the prophets and of all who keep the words of this book. Worship God!*

> (Revelation 22:8–9)

3. Witnesses to the resurrection: the five hundred

In his letter to the Christians at Corinth, written about AD 55, Paul supplies a summary of the appearances of Jesus. It is not intended to be a complete list, but he mentions the appearance to Peter and to the apostles, and concludes with his own encounter with Jesus, recorded in Acts 9, and repeated by Paul as his testimony in Acts 22 and again in Acts 26. He also refers to an appearance of Jesus to five hundred people at once, and comments that most of them were still alive (and so available as witnesses) when Paul wrote the letter, some twenty years later.

We don't know much about this group of people. We do know that Jesus was accompanied by the twelve disciples during the three or so years when he was teaching, and also that there was a larger group of seventy followers whom he sent out on mission (Luke 10:1–20). Luke also mentions a group of 120, who met together in Jerusalem, and were responsible for appointing a replacement for Judas (Acts 1:12–26). But clearly there were more followers of Jesus than these: the church was already growing rapidly, perhaps as news of the resurrection appearances of Jesus spread. Now there were five hundred more voices to say with confidence: 'We have seen Jesus, alive from the dead.'

4. Belief and unbelief

Over the years there has been a steady flow of books claiming to tell us what '*really*' happened: at the birth of Jesus . . . when he walked on the sea of Galilee . . . when the five thousand were fed . . . at the resurrection. In 1995 yet another appeared.

'What *Really* Happened to Jesus?' is subtitled 'a historical approach to the resurrection'. According to the author, Gerd Ludemann, the appearance to the five hundred happened on the Day of Pentecost; it was in fact the Pentecost event. To me this suggestion seems simply unscholarly and certainly not historical. There simply is no evidence for it. The only number remotely connected with Pentecost is the 120 of the group mentioned in Acts 1, and the event of Pentecost has nothing whatever to do with an appearance of *Jesus*, but is the empowering of the church by the *Spirit*.

The appearances went on for forty days, each appearance strengthening the faith of the first Christians. The Jesus whom they now encountered was the same Jesus they had known before, but yet infinitely greater. He could do what he could do before: speak to them, recognize them, he could even eat with them (Luke 24:42). He was sometimes, it seems, invisibly present, as when he heard Thomas stating the conditions he attached to belief, but when he appeared physically to them he was not a ghost, a cloud, or an emanation. He had a material body: he had flesh and bones (Luke 24:39). In fact it seems that the risen Christ retained all the powers he had before his death, but they were augmented, added to, increased – he could do *more*.

Professor Kingsley Barrett summarizes this aspect of the resurrection in his commentary on John's gospel:

> The resurrection has made possible a new and more spiritual union between Jesus and his disciples; the old physical contacts are no longer appropriate, though touch may yet be appealed to in proof that the glorified Lord is none other than he who was crucified.
>
> (*The Gospel According to St John*, p. 470)

It must be emphasized that the disciples of Jesus were *not* expecting the resurrection. Mary and the others went to the rock tomb in order to complete the anointing of the body of Jesus. And when they told the apostles that the tomb was empty, and that angelic messengers at the tomb had told them that Jesus was risen, the apostles simply didn't believe them: 'these words seemed to them like nonsense' (Luke 24:12). When at last the apostles *were* convinced because Jesus appeared to *them*, Thomas, who wasn't there, refused to believe them. John sums up this total lack of expectancy:

> *They still did not understand from Scripture that Jesus had to rise from the dead.*

> (John 20:9)

But the tomb was empty, the body was gone, and a living Jesus had been seen by witnesses who were very hard to convince.

Various groups of people have offered various explanations of the events. The men who had been put to guard the tomb were ordered, apparently by the Sanhedrin itself, to say that the disciples had come in the night while they were asleep, and stole the body (Matthew 28:11–15). It is almost impossible to believe that the whole guard would dare to sleep on duty, and quite impossible that they should all be so sound asleep that not one of them heard the noise that must have been made if the great stone was rolled away from the tomb so that the disciples could get in. And how could sleeping soldiers know that the disciples were the robbers?

Some modern writers have naively suggested that

the women did not even know which was the right tomb, so that the words, 'He is not here', come to mean, 'He is not here in *this* tomb', and, 'See the place where he lay' are said to have been accompanied by a hand gesture indicating *another* tomb. It's a neat argument but it simply dismisses the part of the statement that blows the 'explanation' sky high. The words were: 'He is not here; *for he has risen* as he said. Come, see the place where he lay' (Matthew 28:6). In any case, it would be extraordinary for the women not to know where the tomb was: we are told that after Joseph of Arimathea had rolled the stone before the door of the rock cave Mary Magdalene and the other Mary were there 'sitting opposite the tomb' (Matthew 27:61).

The Ahmadi sect of Islam (which only appeared in the early twentieth century) have another theory. They say that Jesus was taken down from the cross alive, and was revived in the tomb by Joseph of Arimathea, who in their explanation becomes a skilled doctor, using the anointing spices that he had brought with him. In the cool of the tomb these produced a strange interaction, and restored Jesus' breathing. He revived, somehow freed himself from the cloths in which he had been wrapped, but then found himself naked. He couldn't go out like that, but 'He solved the problem very simply. He found the garments of a gardener – most likely in a garden shed nearby – borrowed them and went into town and obtained more suitable clothing. Later he returned the gardener's outfit.' This extraordinary nonsense appears in *Deliverance from the Cross*, written by Muhammad Zafrulla Khan, and first published by the London Mosque in 1978. It is a good indication of the lengths some people will go to in order to discredit the resurrection of Jesus. As the author rightly says:

> Once it is established that Jesus did not die upon the cross, there was no accursed death, no bearing of the sins of mankind, no resurrection, no ascension and no atonement. The entire structure of church theology is thereby demolished. Paul, who was the real founder of church Christianity, said: 'For I delivered unto you first of all that which I also received, how that Christ died for our sins according to the Scriptures; and that he was buried, and that he rose again the third day according to the Scriptures . . . . if Christ is not risen, then is our preaching vain and your faith is also vain' (1 Cor.15:3–4, 14).

At this point we too will consider why the resurrection of Jesus is so vital.

5. The importance of the resurrection

For Christian faith the resurrection of Jesus is not an optional extra. It is vital, central. Paul emphasizes this in his first letter to the Christians at Corinth, allocating an entire chapter to a discussion of the resurrection (chapter 15). Apparently there were already some Christians who, like the Sadducees, did not believe in any resurrection of the dead. Paul lists seven consequences that flow from a denial of the resurrection:

1. 'Christ has not been raised': he is still dead (v.13 and again in v.16).
2. 'Our preaching is useless' (v.14), because those first preachers focused on Christ crucified and risen from the dead.

3. 'Our faith is useless' (v.14), because if there is no resurrection then Christ is dead and he is *not* 'Son of God in power'. Paul repeats this in v.17: '. . . your faith is futile'.

4. Christian preachers such as Paul 'misrepresent God' (v.15), by preaching that God raised Jesus from the dead.

5. We are 'still in our sins' (v.17). The sacrifice made by Christ was in vain: he died, but that's all. His death was not accepted as atoning for sin; God did not raise him from death.

6. Christians who have 'died trusting in Christ' have perished like him (v.18).

7. Christians are 'of all people most to be pitied' (v.19). They accept persecution and hardship in this life because they are trusting in Christ and hope for heaven, but if there is no heaven they have no fun here and will have none there.

In fact the resurrection is the test of everything that Jesus said and promised. According to Mark, the earliest of the gospel writers, Jesus told his followers he would be killed but would rise again and come back to life (Mark 9:31 and 10:34). Mark comments:

> *They did not understand what he meant, and were afraid to ask him about it.*

(Mark 9:32)

Here was the ultimate test of all that Jesus claimed to be. Others had offered new explanations of the mystery of life. Other religions had been founded. Miracles had been performed – even Pharaoh's magicians back in the days of Moses had been able to perform miracles! But here was the ultimate test: could Jesus beat death? Not cheat it, escape from it, but face up to it, accept it, and overcome it, conquer it. The crucifixion meant either the end of Jesus as Saviour and Lord or it meant the end of death as the last enemy. He either stayed in the tomb, one more discredited Messiah, or he rose from the dead. The resurrection is crucial to Christianity.

6. Preaching the resurrection

The preaching of the first Christians seems to have focused more on the resurrection of Jesus than on his death. Everyone believed that Jesus had died on that cross. The real question to be answered was: did he rise from the dead? After the treachery and death of Judas, when Matthias was chosen to replace him, the new apostle's task was to 'become with us *a witness to his resurrection*' (Acts 1:22). Speaking on the Day of Pentecost, Peter said: 'This Jesus *God raised up*, and of that we all are witnesses' (Acts 2:32). When Peter and John healed a man crippled from birth, Peter told the crowd: '. . . you . . . killed the Author of life, whom *God raised from the dead*. To this we are witnesses' (Acts 3:15). Acts 4 describes the witness of the apostles, and Luke comments that 'with great power the apostles gave their testimony to *the resurrection of the Lord Jesus*' (v.33). When Peter and the apostles were arrested, thrown into prison, miraculously released from prison and then re-arrested they told the Sanhedrin:

The God of our fathers raised Jesus whom you killed by hanging him on a tree. God exalted him at his right hand as Leader and Saviour . . . and we are witnesses to these things.

(Acts 5:30–32)

Right at the beginning of his letter to the church at Rome Paul emphasizes that Jesus was 'descended from David according to the flesh and designated Son of God in power . . . *by his resurrection from the dead*' (Romans 1:3–4).

7. Resurrection and the Christian hope

The resurrection was central to the thinking and the teaching and the preaching and the living of the first Christians. The resurrection gave them hope, assurance, confidence that death was not the end of everything. The Bible *does* speak in terms of *bodily* resurrection, not merely of continuing existence as a kind of ghost, a sort of cosmic amoeba, after death. Those first disciples of Jesus were convinced of the truth of all that Jesus had said by two things: the appearances of Jesus, alive, and the empty tomb.

In order to explode the whole story of Christianity, to kill it off before it had even begun, the Jewish authorities needed to do just one thing – produce the body of Jesus. They didn't, because they couldn't. His body was gone.

BUT *we shall be seriously wrong if we assume that the 'resurrection body' is simply the body we may have now, but set free from any further illness.*

As we have already seen, the resurrection body of Jesus had all the powers of his body *before* his crucifixion and resurrection – *and more*. Christianity affirms that my life after death will not be the life of a shapeless spirit, but of me with a new kind of body, what Paul calls a 'spiritual' body.

He deals with the question of the spiritual body in 1 Corinthians 15, a chapter we have already looked at because of what it says about the importance of the resurrection of Jesus. Paul recognized that people would naturally want to know what they would look like in this new resurrection life. So he puts this important question to himself: 'How are the dead raised? With what kind of body do they come?' And he has an answer:

> *What you sow does not come to life unless it dies. And what you sow is not the body which is to be, but a bare kernel, perhaps of wheat or of some other grain. But God gives it a body as he has chosen, and to each kind of seed its own body.*

> (1 Corinthians 15:36–38)

In my time I have grown thousands of eucalyptus trees. They grew very easily in Ethiopia. You simply take the small nuts which grow on the tree, put them out in the sun to let them dry. Then they break open, and out pour the seeds, maybe a hundred inside each nut. Tiny black spheres. Sow them, cover them with a thin layer of soil, water them, and in days the seeds begin to shoot, in a few years you have ... enormous black spheres? No! Instead, from those rather ugly, uninteresting tiny round black seeds you get towering, magnificent, shimmering eucalyptus trees. The first lesson to be learned from this seed and tree imagery is that the tree is unimaginably more wonderful than the seed. Yet, secondly, all the wonder of the tree is hidden there in the seed. Thirdly, there is a one-to-one connection between each seed and each tree. No two seeds are exactly alike and no two trees are exactly alike, but each tree corresponds precisely to its own seed. I believe this is what Paul had in mind when he wrote to the Christians at Colossae, '*Your life is hid with Christ in God. When Christ who is our life appears, then you will appear with him* in glory' (Colossians 3:3–4). We may think that we are attractive, even beautiful, when we are young, but that fades all too quickly. Christians, however, should grow *spiritually*, almost in proportion to the way in which they *diminish* in beauty on the outside. And the hope is that that inward beauty, invisible in the seed, will be revealed in the life beyond, in heaven, in my new spiritual body.

In turn that leads me to expect that we will know one another in that life beyond this. Our bodies will have none of the weaknesses they have now, but all of the powers they have now, *plus*. And if now I can recognize my friends, my family, surely I shall be able to do so then. Especially as *their* new bodies, like mine, will all have that one-to-one relationship to the bodies left behind, transformed, resurrected, in Christ.

Paul actually gives us a little more detail about these resurrection bodies. He contrasts the bodies we have now with the bodies we will have then: they are now physical, they will be spiritual; they are weak, they will be powerful; they are perishable, they will be imperishable; they are 'dishonourable', ugly and weak, they will be 'glorious', beautiful and strong.

The Old Testament
Right through the Old Testament we find very little said about life beyond the grave. Certainly the people of the Old

Testament believed that there was life beyond the grave. In fact so far no people has yet been found that did *not* believe in life beyond the grave. But the Jews did not know anything about it. To them it was a shadow, a dark mystery. The dead were out there, somewhere, in *Sheol* (in *The Pit*), alive, but to be left alone, and certainly not to be envied. They could from time to time come back to this world, as the prophet Samuel did (1 Samuel 28), but if they did then it was best to get them back where they belonged, in *Sheol*, with the rest of the dead, not among the living.

Of course the people of Old Testament times could not have known anything much about life after death. That knowledge could only come through Jesus, God incarnate, living, crucified, dead, buried risen and ascended – revealing to us that death has been defeated; promising us eternal life, not merely life like this but going on for ever and ever, a new quality of life, the life of eternity, lived not in our present bodies miraculously propped up century after century, but in new, transformed resurrection bodies, marvellously surpassing our present bodies, and yet wonderfully revealing all the potential God brought into being when he created you and me.

5

New Life

1. New life for the first Christians

The first Christians immediately realized that the resurrection of Jesus was absolutely central to the Good News. Only if Jesus were alive could there be any good news to preach. If death had beaten him then it would continue to beat us. But if he came through then we could come through. His resurrection life had a new quality about it, a new power in it. *This* was eternal life, the life of eternity. Well then, we could have it too.

Right from the start, baptism was the outward sign of admission to the church. When, on the Day of Pentecost, people responded to Peter's first public preaching of the good news and asked, 'What shall we do?' Peter's reply was immediate and very clear: '*Repent and be baptized*' (Acts 2:37–38).

Baptism was a public witness, but it was more than that. It was also an acted parable, a parallel to Christ's death and resurrection, the water representing the grave, death. Before going into the water a person had life of a sort, but their descent into the water symbolized the believer's death, after which they came out of the water to life again, but 'resurrection life', a new quality of life, the life of eternity. It's all explained in Romans 6:3–4:

> *Don't you know that all of us who were baptized into Christ Jesus were baptized into his death? We were therefore buried with him through baptism into death, in order that, just as Christ was raised from the dead through the glory of the Father, we too may live a new life.*

82

This is what we have always needed: power to live a new kind of life; resurrection power which would enable us to defeat temptation, to show love to others, to speak the truth. Christianity is not a mere theory, it is not even a theology, it has at its heart a living Christ, and the power of his resurrection life made available to me! This power is brought to the Christian by the Holy Spirit. We shall be thinking about the Holy Trinity in the next chapter, but we cannot talk about the Christian's new life without referring to the third Person of the Holy Trinity, the Holy Spirit. God the Father we know through Jesus. Jesus we know through the incarnation. The Holy Spirit we come to know as he moves into our lives.

Immediately before he was arrested, Jesus told his followers:

> *It is for your good that I am going away. Unless I go away, the Counsellor will not come to you; but if I go, I will send him to you.*

> (John 16:7)

Jesus' promise is quite clear. He would be arrested, tried, condemned, executed, buried, rise from the dead, ascend to his Father, and from there would send to them the 'Counsellor'. It all happened as he said. He was arrested, tried, executed, buried, rose from death, was seen by his followers, and after forty days he ascended to his Father.

And after a further ten days he sent the Counsellor, the Holy Spirit. We can read about the coming of the Holy Spirit in Acts 2: 1–4:

> *When the Day of Pentecost came* [fifty days after Passover, when Jesus had been crucified] *they were all together in one place. Suddenly a sound like the blowing of a violent wind came from heaven and filled the whole house where they were sitting. They saw what seemed to be tongues of fire that separated, and came to rest on each of them. All of them were filled with the Holy Spirit . . .*

The rest of the book of Acts is essentially an account of what those first Christians did, their '*acts*', which were made possible because they had been filled with the Holy Spirit. Right from the beginning it was quite clear that these first Christians were people of power, not mere talkers. When Jesus had been arrested, Peter had three times denied any connection with him. But after he was filled with the Spirit we see him out in the streets of Jerusalem, openly preaching about Jesus, fearlessly standing up to the threats of the religious leaders, healing the sick, even raising the dead! The change in Peter and the rest was startling. When the religious leaders of the Jews had Peter and John arrested and interrogated them they recognized that something new, something strange, had happened to these fishermen:

> *When they saw the courage of Peter and John and realized that they were unschooled, ordinary men, they were astonished and they took note that these men had been with Jesus.*

(Acts 4:13)

What had happened is simply explained. Before they had been filled with the Holy Spirit they had been much like everyone else: liars when it suited them, sometimes proud, sometimes even violent, unable to be what they wanted to be, unable to do what they wanted to do, unable to control their temper if it was tested too far. There was an inevitability about their behaviour. In fact they were controlled by the operation of a law from which they could not escape. But Christ's death *for* them and the Spirit's coming *to* them had set them free from *that* law and brought them under quite a different law. These two laws are referred to in Romans 8:2 as:

♦ the law of sin and death
♦ the law of the Spirit of life.

2. Two laws

The Christian view of human nature is very clearly set out in a brief passage in Paul's letter to the church at Rome. This is how he describes the frustrations that we have all felt at one time or another:

> *I do not understand my own actions. For I do not do what I want, but I do the very thing I hate . . . I can will what is right, but I cannot do it. For I do not do the good I want, but the evil I do not want is what I do . . . So I find it to be a law that when I want to do right, evil lies close at hand.*
>
> (Romans 7:15–21)

Of course Paul is not saying that we *never* do anything good. But he is talking about the simple fact that frustrates us all: we are not free. There are times when what we do appals us; we hadn't intended doing it, but there it is, that's what we have done. Actually I have never found anyone who disagreed with what Paul has to say here. It is a profound and yet at the same time simple analysis of the human condition.

In fact this analysis is so important that I set it out here in its entirety. I've used the Living Bible paraphrase because it is so very clear:

> I don't understand myself at all, for I really want to do what is right, but I can't. I do what I don't want to – what I hate. I know perfectly well that what I am doing is wrong, and my bad conscience proves that I agree with these laws I am breaking. But I can't help myself, because I'm no longer doing it. It is sin inside me that is stronger than I am that makes me do these evil things.
>
> I know that I am rotten through and through so far as my old sinful nature is concerned. No matter which way I turn I can't make myself do right. I want to but I can't. When I want to do good I don't, and when I try not to do wrong, I do it anyway. Now if I am doing what I don't want to, it is plain where the trouble is: sin still has me in its evil grasp.
>
> It seems to be a fact of life that when I want to do what is right, I inevitably do what is wrong, I love to do God's will so far as my new nature is concerned; but there is something else deep within me, in my lower nature, that is at war with my mind and wins the fight and makes me a slave to the sin that is still within me. In my mind I want to be God's willing servant, but instead I find myself enslaved to sin.
>
> So you see how it is: my new life tells me to do right, but the old nature that is still inside me loves to sin. Oh, what a terrible predicament I'm in! Who will free me from my slavery to this deadly lower nature? Thank God! It has been done by Jesus Christ our Lord. He has set me free.
>
> (Romans 7:15–25)

3. The law of sin and death

So there are two laws, and we operate either under the one or under the other. The *law of sin and death* is the law that relates to what Paul calls the 'evil' within him – and within others. On Wednesday, March 13, 1996 a man walked into a school in Dunblane, Scotland. He carried four guns, and around his shoulders he had bandoleers containing something like five hundred bullets. He made his way purposefully to the gymnasium, where some of the youngest children in the school, five and six-year olds, were having their gym lesson. He killed sixteen of them, and their teacher, wounded six more and two more teachers, and then shot himself. As we heard the news shock was followed by incredulity: how could anyone do that? And then a word was spoken that was used again and again to characterize what had been done. The school's head-teacher used it. The Prime Minister used it. The word was *evil*. And we all knew what people meant by it.

'Evil' is essentially a *religious* word. It reflects a *moral* judgment. But there's more to it than that. Describing the act of the killer as *evil* rather than merely *criminal* reflected the view of almost everyone – that no ordinary human being could shoot down little children in cold blood. Something *evil* took over at Dunblane that Wednesday morning. It was an extreme illustration of what Paul was talking about: evil in me. An alien power that is stronger than I am.

It is this alien power that brings to nothing every humanitarian effort of the United Nations, or even of well-meaning governments. People live mostly under the law of sin and death. Although it is true that we all have moments of kindness and love, when we long for justice, far stronger and more enduring are the times of selfishness and greed, the outbursts of anger, the preoccupation with *me* rather than with *you*, still less with God. This means, for example, that when our governments might see a cut in our living standards as the only way to achieve decent living standards for countries like Somalia and Liberia and Rwanda they know they have no chance of getting us to agree to a cut. Sin shouts 'Me first!'

The problem is not confined to countries like America or Britain, or Germany. It's worldwide. Go to Addis Ababa, to the headquarters of the Organization of African Unity. Count the Mercedes cars lined up outside. Watch the representatives of some of the poorest countries in the world driving off to the luxury hotels for their fabulous meals and you will realize that it's not a white skin that makes us greedy: it's sin, not skin. It's evil that is within us, it's the *law of sin and death*:

♦ I really want to do what is right.
♦ But, I can't.
♦ I know perfectly well that what I am doing is wrong.
♦ But, I can't help myself.
♦ It seems to be a fact of life that when I want to do what is right I inevitably do what is wrong.
♦ The reason is: sin within me.

If that fits in with your experience then you agree with the Christian analysis of the human predicament. That is important, because not all religions agree on this pessimistic view of human nature. Confucius appears to have taught that what we need is freedom to respond naturally to our own natures. Remove the police, take away the rules, be yourself. Islam teaches that although we have a tendency to do what is wrong all we need is the law, the *Sunnah*, to guide us, and if we want to do what is right, to live according to Sunnah, the law, the practice of Muhammad, then we can. The Orthodox Jew is expected to obey the Jewish Law, the Torah, with its 365 prohibitions: one for every day of the year.

In fact a lot of people seem to think that Christianity itself is no more than a set of rules, most of them negative. On the contrary. As Paul says, the law merely serves to make me worse. Here is what he says about covetousness – wanting things:

> *I should not have known what it is to covet if the law had not said 'You shall not covet.'*
>
> *But sin, finding opportunity in the commandment, wrought in me all kinds of covetousness.*

(Romans 7:7–8)

Builders used to put up warning signs when painting fences and walls: 'Wet Paint! Do not touch!'. But they don't do that so much now, because that commandment did something to everyone who read it. Somehow they felt an irresistible urge to touch the paint . . . So now the wise painter of fences puts up a different sign: 'Wet Paint! Test here!' and provides the passer-by with a small panel of wet paint so that the rest of the fence will be left alone. The law of sin is as simple, as practical, as relevant as that.

4. The law of the Spirit of Life

The alternative to the law of sin and death is the *law of the Spirit of Life*. It is the new *law* that brings new life to us through the coming of the *Holy Spirit*. When Jesus told his followers he was about to leave them, he explained that this was better for them (John 16:7). Of course at the time it would have been impossible for them to believe that anything could be better than having Jesus himself with them . . . always. But when the Holy Spirit came to them then they could see *why* this was better. For one thing, when Jesus had been with them he could be in only one place at a time. When he was with Peter and James and John up on a mountain in Galilee, he couldn't also be with the rest of his followers who were in desperate need of his help down in the valley, trying to heal a boy whose father had brought him to them (Luke 9:28–43).

The Holy Spirit did not become 'incarnate' as Jesus did. And so he was not limited, as human beings are, to being in one place at a time. He remained the Holy *Spirit*, the third Person of the Holy Trinity, not caught in time, but free in eternity, able to be both here and there and anywhere as he wills, as we need. The Holy Spirit can be – and is – in Galilee and in Jerusalem, in Birmingham and in Madras, in Nairobi and in Lima.

It was the Holy Spirit who 'filled' those same first followers of Jesus at Pentecost, traditionally known as 'Whitsun'. (It came to be known as 'White Sunday' because the early church used to hold mass baptisms of new converts on Pentecost Sunday, when those to be baptized wore clean white clothes to symbolize purity.) At Pentecost Jesus' followers received special power to enable them to begin the task of mission, to preach. Peter at once demonstrated this new power; and the result was three thousand people baptized into the church!

I deliberately wrote 'filled' in that last paragraph, with the quotation marks, because it is important that we don't think of the Holy Spirit as a kind of liquid, used to 'top up' Christians when they begin to lose power. The Holy Spirit is not a spirit like petrol or alcohol, but he is a Person, and when he comes into our lives, perhaps to give us some new task, some new gift, we often feel emotionally full, overflowing. So the imagery of being 'filled' is fine, but it *is* only imagery.

The law of the Spirit of Life means that our lives are no longer limited by such gifts as we inherited from our parents. We might be artistic, or mathematical, or good at teaching, or patient, *naturally*. But the Spirit can give us *spiritual* gifts: a gift of teaching, for example, which is different from the natural gift of teaching. It is a gift which does more than help people to learn facts: it helps people to change attitudes, to repent, to love God, to pray. But the new law of the Spirit of Life is a law which applies to the whole of our lives. The law of sin and death says that we *will* sin, but the law of the Spirit of Life says that we don't *have* to.

But once again we need to be very careful in the way we think about this new law. The new law doesn't say that we *can't* sin, only that we don't *have* to sin. We sometimes excuse some sin of ours by saying that the temptation was too great. Well, it wasn't! As Paul had to say to the church at Corinth, where some appalling things were going on amongst the members:

> *No temptation has overtaken you but such as normally comes to people.*
> *God is faithful, and he will not let you be tempted beyond your strength, but with the temptation will also provide the way of escape, that you may be able to endure it.*

(1 Corinthians 10:13)

Sometimes the way of escape may be in the circumstances of the temptation: a knock at the door, a phone call, a sudden storm so that we can't go out . . . and so we don't do what we had planned to do. But often the way of escape is the Holy Spirit who brings to mind something said in church, reminds us of some word spoken by Jesus, sharpens our conscience. He has so many ways of bringing into play this new law of the Spirit of Life.

Let us be quite clear about one thing, however: although this law does not *compel* us to live lives of obedience to God, doing what is right, not doing what is wrong, still Christianity actually *is* all about 'making us good'. As S.H. Travis reminds us (*New Dictionary of Theology*, IVP, p.322): 'a Christian's hope is not utopian. He expects progress, but not perfection . . .' But we *do* expect progress. If Christianity can't produce good people then it is a sham. Ultimately the aim *is* perfection, maturity: as Paul put it he wanted to have everyone *mature in Christ* (Colossians 1:28).

As I write this, I have just been to a very unusual funeral service. It was for Sue, the wife of a local minister, a former student of London Bible College. A fellow student, Becky, spoke of the time when they had shared a house together, and of Sue's habit of having the occasional 'practising for heaven' day, when the whole day was given over to imagining heaven, talking about heaven, behaving as one might behave in heaven. You might imagine that Sue was super-spiritual; but really she was just someone who took heaven seriously and wanted to be prepared for it. Sue died at the age of 35. But what a funeral that was as we heard more and more of what her heavenly-mindedness had done for her husband, her family, her church, her friends. She lived in the light of heaven.

We expect progress though not perfection. We grow towards perfection as the Spirit steadily shows us his views on right and wrong, as he sets us free from old sins . . . and then goes on to point out new sins that must be dealt with. Sin is a bit like an onion. An onion won't bring any tears to your eyes until it is opened up. Take the outer skin off, and then the next layer, and the next, and as you go deeper in so the more the tears flow. To change the metaphor, God is like a fire, and the closer you get to the fire so the hotter the fire feels. The closer you get to God, the more the contrast between our idea of what is good and his becomes more apparent.

Sin! It's not just a vague theological idea, but an essential word to describe a reality. I was in London's Soho. A woman came out of a shop, dragging her child after her. He was maybe four years old, obviously terrified. As she dragged him off down the street, sobbing, she was shouting at him: 'I'll kill you when I get you home.' That's sin, sin that had that child's life in ruins before it had even had a chance to flower into something beautiful for God. But that's not all. What about the sin that had ruined the young woman's own life? What had turned her life into such a hell? Just a few years before she had been a girl at school, playing with the other girls, running home at the end of each day to her mother, her father . . . Or was it they who had marred her life? Or perhaps her marriage? I don't know, but I do know that that's what sin does to us. And it takes Jesus to mend us.

When I was student pastor of a church in the poorer part of Woolwich I used to visit people on Sunday afternoons, among them one couple who were past coming out, but passed all their time in their little home. He told me their story. He had been a rough, tough, drunken sort of a man, and on a Saturday night he had often beaten his wife for no reason except that he was fighting drunk. He ruined her health. Then he became a Christian. Converted, turned round, he began to live a new life. His concern now was to try to make up to his wife for all the wasted years: his life was dedicated to caring for her. Sin *can* be beaten.

5. Becoming a Christian

The Spirit doesn't make us into new people without our consent. The God who reveals himself in the Bible has given us the dignity and the responsibility of making our own decisions.

If we wish we can keep him out of our lives altogether. We can do this. Perhaps the thought of having him there – in our home, listening to our conversation, watching us fill in the income tax form and the lottery tickets; at work, watching the way we behave there – may all seem just too much. Having him there would certainly demand a few changes in the way we do things. And we don't want to make those changes.

But what if we *do* want to make the changes. What if all that has been argued in this book makes sense, what if you do want to start over? What then? What must I do to move on from the law of sin and death to the law of the Spirit of Life?

6. Becoming a Christian: what must I do?

First of all, the answer to this question is not 'Nothing'. 'Nothing' is what I have to do if I want to stay the way I am. Secondly it's worth noting that if I do want to move on into this new kind of life, this in itself is evidence that God is already at work, seeking me. It is he who has put this wish into my mind.

In case you find this difficult to understand, let me explain. In his book *Christianity Rediscovered*, Vincent Donovan, a missionary amongst the Maasai people in northern Kenya, tells how the Maasai taught him the real meaning of faith. In explaining to the Maasai how to become a Christian he had used a Maasai word which meant 'to agree to', rather as you might 'agree to' the analysis of human life that I have suggested in this book. A Maasai elder put him straight:

> He said for a man really to believe is like a lion going after its prey. His nose and eyes and ears pick up the prey. His legs give him the speed to catch it. All the power of his body is involved in the terrible death leap and single blow to the neck with the front paw, the blow that actually kills. And as the animal goes down the lion envelops it

in his arms (Africans refer to the front legs of an animal as its arms), pulls it to himself, and makes it part of himself. This is the way a lion kills. This is the way a man believes. This is what faith is.

That's part of the explanation of what faith is. But the Maasai elder continued:

You told us of the High God, how we must search for him, even leave our land and our people to find him. But we have not done this. We have not left our land. We have not searched for him. He has searched for us. He has searched us out and found us. All the time we think we are the lion. In the end the lion is God.

That's the second part of the explanation of what faith is. Ultimately even faith is God's gift to us:

It is by grace you have been saved, through faith – and this is not from yourselves, it is the gift of God.

(Ephesians 2:8)

7. Becoming a Christian: six vital steps

Although ultimately it is God who gives us faith, still the answer to the question 'What must I do?' is not 'Nothing.' New life won't come simply by passively waiting for it to arrive, waiting for the lion to pounce. So here are six ways in which the New Testament answers the question 'What must I do?'

(i) I must believe

I have to accept God's explanation of this world, his explanation of why life is so unsatisfactory and how Christ's death can put me right. I must believe in Jesus, accepting that he is more than a prophet, more than a teacher, more than a worker of miracles. We must accept Jesus as Thomas did: '*My Lord and my God*' (John 20:28).

But belief is more than saying yes to a collection of theological propositions. Belief takes in the consequences of belief, the recognition that if I believe in God's explanation of the world's problems, and if I believe in Jesus as Lord and God then certain consequences must follow: if I really believe then my life will change to match my belief.

(ii) I must be born again

This reflects what Jesus told Nicodemus, a Jewish rabbi. Like so many religious people Nicodemus thought that everyone else had to answer this question 'What must I do?', but that he himself had no need to do anything. Jesus told him bluntly '*You must be born again.*' We all need a fresh start, and only God can give it to us. Becoming a Christian is like being born again, like starting life again, and this time as a new person.

(iii) I must repent

Repentance means a change of mind, it means regret for the past, it means determining to do things differently, it means recognizing that our selfish and thoughtless ways were wrong, they broke God's laws, and rightly deserve punishment. No excuses! No cover-up! I was wrong. Repentance involves confession (*homologein* literally means 'saying the same thing'), saying the same thing about my sins as God says about them.

(iv) I must give up everything

Jesus put it starkly:

He who loves father or mother more than me is not worthy of me; and he who loves son or daughter more than me is not worthy of me; and he who does not take up his cross and follow me is not worthy of me. He who finds his life will lose it, and he who loses his life for my sake will find it.

(Matthew 10:37–39)

Jesus has to come first, before everything else and before everyone else. It isn't always easy to become a Christian. If your parents are Jewish, or Muslim, or even atheist it can certainly be difficult to become a Christian and it may even be dangerous. The whole way of life may be affected if a Hindu puts Jesus on an entirely different level from the many gods of Hinduism. The rich may find themselves set to lose a fortune if they come to Christ.

Jesus challenges us to weigh it up. Count the cost! Think it through! Is there something or someone that you can't give up, won't give up, so as to follow Christ? If there is, then 'You can't be my disciple . . . you are not worthy of me.'

(v) I must follow Jesus

This means far more than simply trying to imitate Jesus. After all, he lived in his century and we live in ours. Strictly speaking it really isn't possible to live his way today: we would have to turn the clock back to do so. (This is one of the real difficulties that the Muslim has in trying to follow, literally, the lifestyle of Muhammad. Times change, cultures and customs change, even languages change. You can't turn the clock back and you can't stop the clock.)

Still, I must follow Jesus as Peter and John and James and the rest of them did. Jesus is the Rabbi, and I am the disciple. But it's not the *practices* of Jesus that I must follow, but the *principles* which lie behind those practices. Concern for God comes first – Jesus lived out his life in dependence on his Father, and so must I. Concern for the people around me comes second – concern for the poor, the unimportant. Honesty, integrity. Without embarrassment Jesus shared the good news of the Kingdom with the people he met; somehow, so must I. I am not a follower of Martin Luther, John Calvin, Charles Spurgeon or John Wesley; I am not particularly a Lutheran or a Baptist or a Methodist; I am a follower of Jesus.

(vi) I must receive Christ

Writing about Jesus, John commented:

> *He came to his own home, and his own people received him not. But to all who received him, who believed in his name, he gave power to become children of God.*
>
> (John 1:11–12)

John's picture of Jesus is very clear: he came to the world which was created through him, and he came to the Jewish people who ought to have been his people; but the world largely ignored him and the Jews flatly rejected him (although it is interesting that in fact all of the first few thousand believers were Jews).

Jesus didn't abandon either the Jews or his world: he came and offered his life at the cross, so that we could, in exchange, have new life, a fresh start. The new life comes to anyone who will receive him.

I must believe. I must be born again. I must repent. I must give up everything. I must follow Jesus. I must receive Christ.

It was Easter Sunday, 1947. I was sixteen years old, already out at work, as an office boy in London. Already I knew that life didn't make much sense. In a house in a London suburb, kneeling by a little table, I surrendered to God. I was born again, accepting that new start that Jesus promises. So I began my walk with Jesus.

6

One God

1. One God, but . . .

Not three gods, one God. The Nicene Creed, a statement of belief accepted by the Anglican Church, the Roman Catholic Church, the Eastern Orthodox Church and by most Protestant churches, begins:

I believe in one God.

Christians accept the authority of the Old Testament as well as of the New Testament so that a Christian can stand with a Jew and recite the words of the fundamental statement of Jewish belief, the *Shema* (Hebrew for 'Listen', which is the first word of the statement):

Hear O Israel: the Lord our God is one. Love the Lord your God with all your heart and with all your soul and with all your strength.

(Deuteronomy 6:4–5)

And we can join that Old Testament statement across the centuries to the New Testament; Jesus identified this as the most important of all the commandments (see Mark 12:29). Actually a Christian can also stand alongside the Muslim and repeat the first part of the corresponding statement of the fundamental belief of Islam, taken from the *Kalima*, 'the speaking':

There is no God but God.

However Christians have to add a 'but' when they speak in this way about God because, while we believe that God is one, we find that we can't understand the New Testament without recognizing that God is in some way three as well as one. Christianity has developed a Trinitarian theology: God is one but he is also three, the Holy Trinity, God the Father, God the Son, God the Holy Spirit. Although many theologians have tried to reduce this New Testament theology down to a simple statement that God is one, they have always ended up either by abandoning the New Testament or by returning to belief in a Trinity.

2. Knowing God

God has revealed himself to us in many ways. Perhaps the two most important ways are through Jesus and through creation. We have already looked at what Christians believe about Jesus. What about creation? In Romans 1:20 Paul writes:

> For since the creation of the world God's invisible qualities – his eternal power and divine nature – have been clearly seen, being understood from what has been made.

When we do look around us, at creation, at the world we live in, at the stars, and when we realize that this is just one tiny corner of an immense universe we feel ourselves to be less even than a grain of sand. How could we expect the One who made all that immensity to take any notice of us? In Vincent Donovan's *Christianity Rediscovered* he tells of a visit to an American high school. He asked a group of youngsters to think about who would be affected if something really drastic happened to them – if they were to die, suddenly, for example. One girl asked:

> 'You mean if I committed suicide or something?' Donovan agreed that that was the sort of thing he had in mind. The girl thought for a moment, and then replied: 'Mary, here, and my mother.'

No one else? Just two people? An almost imperceptible ripple on the vast pool of life. Would God notice it?

Creation does reveal God's nature, his power; at the same time it makes us feel our insignificance, our lostness in such a vast universe. It puts God out there, when I need him down here.

I remember talking with some African friends about their old religion. Everything appeared to focus on 'Doressa'. He was the cause of every accident, every illness; he it was who caused the rains to fail and brought famine on their land. Ultimately he it was who brought the death they all dreaded. So it was not surprising that the religion of this people focused on Doressa. They offered him annual sacrifices, and their ritual experts, the shamans, worked hard to ensure that Doressa was content with them. Anthropologists who had studied this people heard only of Doressa. According to their books the people had a belief only in this dark, death-dealing Doressa. But that, it became clear, was not true. They had a belief in another, in Magano, the Great God, the Creator of heaven and earth.

Magano, however, was considered to be far too great to be concerned with them. Having made the world he had retired to his own distant land and had no further dealings with the people he had created. When Christians first reached this people with their Good News they gave the traditional message: Christ had died on the cross for the sins of the world, was buried, raised from death and ascended. But that was not what the Darassan peoples heard. What came through to them was the amazing Good News that Magano had come near! And precisely the same thing happened in Rwanda. The Anglican missionaries preached an orthodox western-style Good News, but the good news the people heard was the news that God had come near.

Sometimes I wonder if we Christians have been at fault here. The gospel we have preached has often served to put God a million miles away from our hearers. And yet they desperately need him *here*. The world has so much pain in it: apparently unending conflict in Somalia, in the Sudan, bitter hatred in the Middle East, abject poverty alongside great wealth in Asia, oppression in South America, rampant materialism in Europe, the despair of the unemployed, the tears of the children, the hopelessness of their parents. Yet the God of whom we speak is out there, somewhere, a million miles away. We may respond to his self-revelation in creation: 'God is great!', '*Allahu akbar!*', but it is difficult to imagine him taking note of us.

And God understands all that. He has revealed himself in another way, through the incarnation, God in human form, truly human, truly God. God makes himself small, small enough to be seen, small enough to be touched, handled, known in an entirely new way. He becomes a speck in a woman's womb, a baby born into a poor family in Palestine, a land trampled underfoot by a foreign power, a homeless refugee in Egypt, a wandering preacher with a mere handful of uninfluential followers, a man denied justice, one more victim of religion, condemned to die on a cross. And Christianity says: '*This* is God! God come near.' The New Testament describes the incarnation like this:

104

> *Who, being in very nature God,*
> *did not consider equality with God something to be grasped,*
> *but made himself nothing, taking the very nature of a servant,*
> *being made in human likeness.*
> *And being found in appearance as a man he humbled himself,*
> *and became obedient to death – even death on a cross.*
>
> (Philippians 2:6–8)

It must have been very difficult for the followers of Jesus. They were – all of them – Jews. They had been brought up to repeat the words of the *Shema*, 'The Lord our God is *one.*' Yet it was quite obvious that Jesus stood in some special relationship to God. Jesus himself explained it to them:

> *'If you really knew me, you would know my Father as well. From now on, you do know him and have seen him.'*
>
> *Philip said, 'Lord, show us the Father and that will be enough for us.'*
>
> *Jesus answered, 'Don't you know me, Philip, even after I have been among you such a long time?*
>
> *Anyone who has seen me has seen the Father. How can you say "Show us the Father"?*
>
> *Don't you believe that I am in the Father and that the Father is in me?'*
>
> (John 15:9–10)

Of course it defies logic. 'The Son in the Father and the Father in the Son.' Like a bottle filled with water and then immersed in the sea: water in the bottle and the bottle in the water. The water is the everywhere-present God. Jesus is God, the Father is God.

It seems to have been the resurrection of Jesus that finally convinced the followers of Jesus that he was not merely a prophet, not just a great teacher, but God incarnate, God come near. As we have seen, Thomas seems to have been the first to express it clearly. He had not been there when Jesus had appeared to the gathered disciples on the resurrection day. But a week later Jesus came to him. He was utterly convinced. Without attempting to work out the theology of what he was saying Thomas put his deepest feelings into the simplest of words, in English just five monosyllables: *'My Lord and my God!'* (John 20:28).

3. God the Holy Spirit

We have already looked at Pentecost, in chapter four. Before his arrest, Jesus had promised that he would send 'another Comforter', a 'Counsellor' (John 15:26). The Counsellor would come, as Jesus had come, sent by the Father. Jesus described him as the 'Spirit of truth' who would lead his people into the truth.

After his resurrection, but before his return to heaven, Jesus again spoke about this coming Counsellor, and told his followers:

> Do not leave Jerusalem, but wait for the gift my Father promised, which you have heard me speak about. For John baptized with water, but in a few days you will be baptized with the Holy Spirit.

(Acts 1:4–5)

Who is this 'Counsellor'? The question is particularly important for Muslims since Islam suggests that Muhammad was the promised Counsellor. However two facts make this interpretation untenable.

First of all, Jesus used the Greek work *paraklêtos*, 'Counsellor'. The word was often used with a legal meaning, for counsel in a court of law. He might be counsel for the prosecution or counsel for the defence. In John 16:8 he is clearly prosecuting counsel:

> *When he comes he will convict the world of guilt in regard to sin and righteousness and judgment.*

Some Muslim writers have confused this word, *paraklêtos*, with a similar Greek word, *periklytos*, meaning 'famous', 'renowned', 'praised', which is also the meaning of the name Muhammad. They have then suggested that Muhammad was the promised Counsellor. But there is no Bible manuscript with the word *periklytos* at this point. In fact the word *periklytos* does not occur anywhere in the New Testament.

Secondly we have to note that Jesus promised his followers that this gift of the Holy Spirit, the Counsellor, would be given to them 'in a few days' (Acts 1:5). That promise certainly fits in well with the coming of the Spirit at Pentecost, ten days or so after Jesus had made the promise. But it simply can't be made to fit the five hundred and forty or so *years* that elapsed before the coming of Muhammad.

4. The Holy Trinity

The idea of the Holy Trinity can perhaps be seen best in three events: creation, incarnation, Pentecost. The opening words of the Bible claim:

In the beginning God created the heavens and the earth . . . .
and the Spirit of God was moving over the face of the waters.

(Genesis 1:1)

At the beginning of John's gospel we read:

In the beginning was the Word,
and the Word was with God, and the Word was God.
He was in the beginning with God;
all things were made through him
and without him was not anything made that was made.

(John 1:1–3)

Paul said much the same, with a similar emphasis:

. . . in him all things were created in heaven and on earth, visible and invisible . . .
all things were created through him and for him.

(Colossians 1:16)

When we come to the incarnation we find that all three persons of the Trinity are involved in the baptism of Jesus. Matthew describes what happened:

As soon as Jesus was baptized, he went up out of the water.
At that moment heaven was opened, and he saw the spirit of God descending like a dove and alighting on him.
And a voice from heaven said, 'This is my Son, whom I love. With him I am well pleased.'

(Matthew 3:16–17)

And when we look at the coming of the Holy Spirit we again find the three persons of the Trinity involved. Jesus said to his followers:

> *I will pray the Father, and he will give you another Counsellor . . .*
>
> (John 14:16)

108

Writing to the Christians at Ephesus, Paul refers to the three persons when he describes how he prays

> *I bow my knees before the Father, from whom every family in heaven and on earth is named,*
> *that according to the riches of his glory he may grant you to be strengthened with might through his Spirit in the inner man*
> *and that Christ may dwell in your hearts through faith . . .*
>
> (Ephesians 3:14–17)

He also makes a powerful statement about the essential unity of Christianity:

> *There is one body and* **one Spirit** *. . . one Lord, one faith, one baptism, one God and Father of all . . .*
>
> (Ephesians 4:4–6)

At the end of Matthew's gospel we find Jesus telling his followers that they are to be missionaries, going into all the world, making new followers and then,

> *baptizing them in the name of the Father and of the Son and of the Holy Spirit.*
>
> (Matthew 28:19)

Through history baptism has been the outward sign of admission into the church: and it has been baptism in the name of the Trinity.

There is no easy way of explaining this idea of the

Trinity. There is a story told of the theologian J.S. Whale, who used to give a series of lectures on the Trinity in one of the Scottish universities. When he had finished the course of lectures he used to ask his students: 'Now have you got it?' Each year there would be one who would reply 'Yes!' – to which Whale invariably responded: 'Well then, you've got it wrong!'

I'm not going to offer some simple explanation of the Trinity. But surely it ought not to surprise us that God should turn out to be much more difficult to explain or understand than maybe we thought when we were children.

C.S. Lewis illustrates the Trinity from mathematics. If we stay in one dimension we have a very simple system, simply a row of dots marking out a line. If we advance to two dimensions then we have two lines, which mark out a

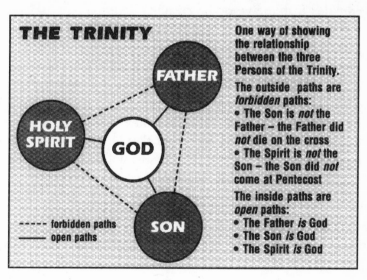

THE TRINITY

FATHER

HOLY SPIRIT

GOD

SON

- - - - - forbidden paths
———— open paths

One way of showing the relationship between the three Persons of the Trinity.

The outside paths are *forbidden* paths:
• The Son is *not* the Father – the Father did *not* die on the cross
• The Spirit is *not* the Son – the Son did *not* come at Pentecost

The inside paths are *open* paths:
• The Father *is* God
• The Son *is* God
• The Spirit *is* God

plane. If we go on to a third dimension we keep all the properties of a line and of a plane, but now we have a solid figure: a cube, a cone or whatever. The form of a cube, for example, has six planes, twelve lines and an infinite number of points and it has the three dimensional property of spaciousness. But then physics reminds us that there is no need to stop there; we can add more dimensions. Admittedly we can't draw them, and most of us can't imagine them, but we can go on adding as many more dimensions as we like. Physics reminds us that time is just another dimension, not at all what we have thought it to be, a comfortable steady sixty seconds to the minute. In fact, just how long your minute is depends on how fast you happen to be travelling. Really! This is a complex world, and it doesn't surprise me at all that God turns out to be even more complex than the world he created.

One final thought about this remarkable idea of the Trinity. On the one hand we can't reduce God to a simple unity. We will always have to say, 'We believe in one God, but . . .' – and yet we must avoid thinking of God as three gods. In Ethiopian art God is often pictured as three identical old men. He isn't three like that. And yet we cannot reject either the statement that God is one or that he is three. The fourth century theologian Gregory of Nazianzus expresses the right balance:

> No sooner do I conceive of the One
> than I am illumined by the splendour of the Three;
> no sooner do I distinguish them
> than I am carried back to the One.

5. God and the three omnis

Theologians often speak about God in terms of the three omnis: that he is omnipresent, everywhere-present; omniscient, all-knowing; and omnipotent, all-powerful. A little thought will suggest that we may need to modify those ideas.

I don't have any particular problem with the idea of God's omnipresence. Psalm 139 expresses the idea very clearly:

Whither shall I go from thy Spirit?
Or, whither shall I fell from thy presence?
If I ascend to heaven, thou art there! If I make my bed in Sheol, thou art there!
If I take the wings of the morning and dwell in the uttermost parts of the sea, even there thy hand shall lead me, and thy right hand shall hold me.
If I say 'Let only darkness cover me, and the light about me be night,' even the darkness is not dark to thee . . . .

So God is omnipresent. Even my sin cannot shut him off from me, although it may well shut me off from him. After all if I am behind with my rent, the landlord is the last person I shall want to meet, although he may be very anxious to see me!

But is God omniscient? Does he know everything? Well, no. I know something that he can never know: I know what it is to be wrong, what it is to sin. Because of the incarnation God knows about sin, and because of the incarnation God knows what it is to be *tempted* by sin. But he doesn't know what it is actually to sin. The philosopher Schleiermacher said that the essence of being human is the feeling of dependence. Well, God doesn't feel that sense of dependence. We might well want to say that within the Holy Trinity there is a perfected sense of dependence – between the Father and the Son, for example. In the incarnation Jesus was perfectly dependent on his Father. But God, the Holy Trinity, is not dependent.

Is God omnipotent? According to Professor James Packer 'God acts in, with and through his creatures so as to do everything that he wishes to do exactly as he wishes to do it' ('God' in the *New Dictionary of Theology*, p.276).

But it seems clear that in reality God doesn't. In Paul's first letter to the Thessalonians he writes – and surely he has got it right:

> . . . *this is the will of God, your sanctification.*

> (1 Thessalonians 4:3)

So am I sanctified? Are you? Well, I am being sanctified, but it certainly hasn't happened yet. But more than that, when we look around this world, do we really see God doing exactly what he wants done? While this book was being written a man burst into a school in Scotland armed with four handguns and shot dead sixteen children, aged five and six years, and their teacher. Was that the will of God? Is cancer the will of God? In 1095 Pope Urban II issued the Appeal of Clermont, calling for a holy crusade against the Muslims, and the liberation of Jerusalem. His watchword was *Deus Vult*, 'God wills it'. But were the Crusades the will of God? The historian Daniel-Rops tells us:

> The conquest of Jerusalem was marked by hideous carnage . . . . at the Mosque of Omar there was such a slaughter that the blood ran ankle deep.

> (*Cathedral and Crusade*, p.446)

Was the Holocaust the will of God?

If all of this expresses the will of an omnipotent God then

we are confronted with a tyrant, a God with whom we can hardly live. But for Christianity God does not write the script. We do. When he created the universe he also created time. Within time he created us, human beings. He created us in his image, free to choose, free to please him or to defy him. He chose to allow this in order that we could really be free, answerable to him because of our freedom. And within time God is *not* omnipotent. The idea that God is omnipotent even within time is a Muslim, not a Christian belief. It is in Islam that Allah writes the script, indeed, writes it down in the Preserved Tablet, leaving us with the duty of submission to it. For Islam, if there is an earthquake, with many dead, as happened in Iran in 1993, then this is the will of Allah, and it is for us to submit. But that is *not* Christian teaching.

God is *not* on the throne. It is the task of Christians to put him on the throne: in their own lives, first; in the life of the church, next; and then, through their struggles in a fallen world, in the society around them.

But there is one last word to say. If God is not enthroned here, he is enthroned in eternity. Christians pray, 'Thy will be done on earth, *as it is in heaven.*' At the beginning of time the omnipotent God freely created us and created us free. At the end of time God calls us all to judgment, to answer for the kind of lives we have lived. And along the way, within time, God has placed markers to remind us: 'I am here'. The Exodus. The Exile. The incarnation, Pentecost, the very occasional miracles. These are all his markers. They remind us: 'Within time you may choose to go your own way. But I am here. And it is given to all humanity to die, once. After this comes judgment.'

7

Taking God's Word for it

1. The Bible: a special history

The Bible is really a library of sixty-six assorted books, poems and letters. It is possible to sort out the historical books from the rest and so to obtain a reasonably continuous outline of history *as the writers of the Bible saw it. The Bible does give us a history of the world, but it is a history seen from a very special viewpoint.* Here are one or two examples from the Old Testament. The Battle of Carchemish, in 605 BC, an event of great international significance when Babylon smashed the power of Egypt, is passed over with scarcely a mention. Militarily great kings, such as Omri, may be given passing reference, while the lives of men like King Ahab, of almost no significance beyond his own land, are recorded in great detail. The writers were not interested in politics so much as in morals, not so much in charting the conflicts between the nations as in detailing the conflict between kings and prophets. The result is history from a special point of view.

Of course that is true of every so-called history. What has traditionally been taught in schools as 'history' is merely the history of political power, usually presented as if it were the history of humankind. But, as Karl Popper made shatteringly clear in his book *The Open Society and its Enemies* (vol. 2, p.70) the history of power politics is one of international crime and mass murder, in which some of the greatest criminals are extolled as heroes.

The history found in the Bible is very different. It is largely a history of unimportant people and an insignificant nation, through whom God has gradually disclosed a plan of salvation for the world. The process of revealing this plan of salvation passes through two distinct phases, corresponding roughly to the Old Testament period and the New Testament period, relating firstly to the Old Testament people of God, Israel, and secondly to the New Testament people of God, the church.

Frederick the Great is said to have asked his chaplain for proof of the existence of God. According to the story, the chaplain's answer was: 'The Jews.' Certainly the Jews are a remarkable people. For various reasons they seem to have been singled out for persecution century after century, with some six million dying through the terror of the Holocaust, the Nazi persecution around the time of the Second World War. And despite all this persecution the Jews are still with us, still a distinct people, a nation. The Old Testament is primarily concerned with their history. They were to be God's witnesses, his servants, his messengers, to share their knowledge of him with the surrounding nations. Jerusalem was to have at its heart not a palace but a temple, a temple of such magnificence that the nations would flock into Jerusalem to see it, to be awed by it, to find God through it. This temple would be different from the myriad others

115

in the world: it would contain no image, no statue, of Yahweh.

However, the Old Testament suggests that, with few exceptions, the Jewish people generally thought only in terms of their special privilege. Yes, God was their God, and their history showed that over the centuries he had watched over the nation; doubtless he would continue to do so. In the meantime politics was much more exciting. So they lost sight of God's purpose in calling them.

Isaiah 65 has a striking illustration of God's unsuccessful attempts to get their attention, to call them back to their task. It is a striking, a daring analogy: children playing hide and seek; but the children have given up looking, they are simply not interested in finding God:

> *I revealed myself to those who did not ask for me;*
> *I was found by those who did not seek me.*
> *To a nation that did not call on my name, I said*
> *'Here am I, here am I.'*

(Isaiah 65:1)

Using the more familiar picture of the shepherd, Ezekiel condemns the nation's leaders:

> *The weak you have not strengthened, the sick you have not healed, the crippled you have not bound up, the strayed you have not brought back, the lost you have not sought, and with force and harshness you have ruled them . . . thus says the Lord God: Behold I, I myself, will search for my sheep, and will seek them out.*

(Ezekiel 34: 4–11)

It was with these people that God had made a covenant, an agreement: they would be his people and he would be their

God. He would reveal himself especially to them, so that they could share that knowledge with their neighbours. Through all their long history of rebellion, idolatry, compromise, despite leaders who merely led the people astray and despite the nation's choosing leaders who would inevitably lead them astray, still steadily, God kept the covenant.

117

His justice meant that from time to time there would be punishment for the Jewish peoples. The Exile, when the remnant of the twelve tribes were swept off to Babylon and Jerusalem was left abandoned, in ruins, was clear enough confirmation of that. But God's purpose never wavered: through this people he would bring salvation into the world.

2. The character of God

Throughout the pages of the Bible we are steadily introduced to the character of God. He is a God of

Love. This is a different kind of love from anything we are familiar with. In Deuteronomy Moses muses on why God chose Israel, and he tells the people:

> *It was not because you were more in number than any other people that the Lord set his love upon you and chose you, for you were the fewest of all peoples; but it is because the Lord loves you.*

(Deuteronomy 7:7–8)

So why did God love them? Simply because. Because he loved them! Not because they were a powerful nation, not because they were a religious nation, not because they were an honest, kindly nation. Just because. That is the essence of God's love for us: it is *unconditional love*.

Justice. Alongside God's love there is justice. At the end of each human life and at the end of the story of this world there must be justice. Sometimes (as Israel discovered in the Exile) we meet up with God's justice *now*. But that perfect justice doesn't necessarily come to us in our lifetime. There is a judgment to be faced, beyond this life.

Compassion. This is perhaps best demonstrated in Jesus, who saw the crowds of ordinary people, with so many burdens, so many anxieties, and no idea of where to go for help . . . and Jesus had compassion on them (Matthew 9:36).

Grace. In the Bible, grace means undeserved kindness. God's grace ensures that we don't get what we deserve. Grace allows the sun to shine on the good and the bad (Matthew 5:45). The fact that '*while we were yet sinners Christ died for us*' (Romans 5:8) demonstrates both the love and the sheer grace of God.

Holiness. Perhaps this is one thing about God that we tend to forget: he is holy, different, unlike us, pure, shining, squeaky-clean *good*. We don't know anyone or anything else that has this characteristic. Holiness is the opposite of ordinary, common, human sinfulness.

It is within these characteristics that God becomes also a God of salvation. He works within his own nature to find a way in which he can be just and yet be a God of grace; holy and yet show compassion.

3. The New Testament

The last voice we hear in the Old Testament is that of Malachi, and then there is a silence of almost five hundred years before another prophet appears on the scene: John-the-Baptizer. There is a connection between the two. The closing words of Malachi predict the coming of 'Elijah', and Jesus himself said that John was that 'Elijah' (Matthew 11:7–14).

We would expect great changes to have taken place in the land of Israel over a period of five hundred years. Try to think of the difference between the England of 1490, and the England of 1990. Five hundred years ago the Wars of the Roses had just come to an end at the Battle of Bosworth, when King Richard III was killed, and Henry VII became King of England.

Five hundred years make a lot of difference. For Israel the big difference was the emergence of the Roman Empire, of which Judea was a very minor part, and within Judea the development of the synagogues and the emergence of the religious parties, the Scribes and the Pharisees and the Sadducees.

But what was important about this new era was the emergence of the New Covenant promised centuries earlier by Jeremiah (Jeremiah 31:31–34). It was to be a covenant which made the *meaning* of the Old Covenant clear: all the laws, all the sacrifices, all the annual feasts like Tabernacles and Passover and Pentecost would be explained.

Actually we make two mistakes with our Bibles: we either assume that as Christians we need not pay much attention to the Old Testament at all (whereas it is simply impossible to understand the New Testament without it); or else we try to treat both parts of the Bible equally, so that we run into difficulties with things like the *lex talionis* (the law of retribution – 'an eye for an eye and a tooth for a tooth', sabbath laws, and laws about what food we can eat.

In the Old Testament times Israel was a nation, and so for much of its history it had a king to rule over it. The church has no human ruler; we look to Jesus as Head of the church.

And while Israel was a nation with its own territory and its own language, the church is spread throughout the world, with a multitude of languages, and throughout time.

As a nation Israel needed civil and criminal laws; laws to deal with theft and murder, for example. The church lives under the laws made by secular governments. This is another point at which Christianity differs from Islam, which has its own civil and criminal laws – allowing, for example, up to four wives, and prescribing amputation of the hand for theft.

The Old Testament dealt with sin through animal sacrifices: annual sacrifices and occasional sacrifices to deal with particular sins. Thoughtful people realized that those sacrifices could not really deal with sin (Hebrews 10:4). For the church, one effective sacrifice for sin has been made through the death of Christ, so that there is no longer any need for animal sacrifices.

As a consequence we find that some of the Old Testament laws and practices have been fulfilled in Christ and some are no longer relevant because the church is not a nation.

To take one important example, Israel as a nation was promised that if it was faithful to its covenant with God then it would prosper, and warned that if it were not faithful then it would suffer. This is set out concisely in Deuteronomy 11:13–15:

> *If you will obey my commandments which I command you this day, to love the Lord your God, and to serve him with all your heart and with all your soul, he will give the rain for your land in its season, the early rain and the later rain, that you may gather in your grain and your wine and your oil. And he will give grass in your fields for your cattle and you shall eat and be full.*

If they were not faithful then they would not prosper. We find the same idea again, in more detail, in Leviticus 26 and in Deuteronomy 28. But prosperity is not what is promised to the church. On the contrary, as Paul warned Timothy, '*All who desire to live a godly life in Christ Jesus will be persecuted*' (2 Timothy 3:12). Paul himself said that he had lost everything (Philippians 3:8). The fact is that the New Covenant is not an all-risks-covered insurance policy. Being a Christian does not guarantee a life free of suffering. Christians are unemployed, Christians have terrible accidents, Christians die of cancer, Christians even starve to death. We share these hard experiences *as Christ shared them.* That is the nature of the New Testament, the New Covenant. But of course our reward is not here but there!

4. The Bible is inspired

The Bible is not merely the chance collection of the religious writings and records of a particular nation. It is an inspired book. We must look carefully at what we mean when we say that it is 'inspired'. After all, most religions have their own sacred books, the Qur'an for Muslims, the Upanishads for Hindus, the 'Three Baskets' for Buddhists.

122

First, Christians do believe that the idea of inspiration puts the contents of the Bible back beyond the human writers and into the hand of God. Second, Christians do not believe in a 'dictated' Bible. The Greek of Romans is quite different from the Greek of John's gospel, for example. Paul's personality can be seen in Romans and the different personality of John is seen in his gospel. The authors of the different books each contribute something personal. By contrast, for Islam Muhammad is *not* the author of the Qur'an. He provides the voice through which the Qur'an is transmitted, but no more than that.

We must also point out the danger of quoting verses of the Bible out of their context. Not everything in the Bible is true. To take just two examples, the Bible says, 'Let us eat and drink, for tomorrow we die' (1 Corinthians 15:32), and also that 'one fate comes to all, to the righteous and the wicked, to the good and the evil, to the clean and the unclean, to him who sacrifices and him who does not sacrifice. As is the good man so is the sinner' (Ecclesiastes 9:2). Both of these verses have to be understood in their context, otherwise we will seriously misunderstand them.

But the Bible is inspired. Notice the remarkable way in which the creation story in the first book of the Bible, Genesis 2, with its account of the Tree of Life and of a river flowing out of Eden has its parallel in Revelation 22, the last book of the Bible, where the Tree of Life is multiplied and the river becomes the River of the Water of Life. Notice that in the gospels we have only some of the events in the life of Jesus. John actually says that if everything were to be written down probably the whole world would be unable to contain the resultant library! But John has selected, *under the guidance of the Holy Spirit*, those events which might bring the reader to faith in Christ (John 20:31 and 21:25). Again, the Bible contains two letters written by Paul to the Christians at Corinth, but in the first of those letters he says 'I wrote to you in my letter . . .', which implies that he must have written at least three letters to them.

The Bible is inspired and it is also accurate. I must add that it is reliable only if it is correctly interpreted; it is not a collection of 'proof texts'. In addition, there are some problems with this idea of the accuracy of the Bible. Sometimes the Bible seems to contradict what we know from other sources. For example it used to be thought that Jesus could not have grown up in Nazareth because archaeologists had found no evidence that the town of Nazareth had any settlement before the fourth century AD. The idea of Jesus coming from Nazareth, said some scholars, came from confusion over two texts:

Numbers 6:1–21 spoke of a Nazirite as a class of holy man, and it was suggested that the word Nazirite had become confused with Nazarene. Another suggestion was based on the fact that Isaiah 11:1 refers to a promised deliverer as 'The Branch' (*nitser* in Hebrew), and this word, it was suggested, had been confused with Nazarene.

But in 1955 archaeologists who were excavating beneath

the Church of the Annunciation in Nazareth found clear evidence that in fact the site had been occupied even *before* the Christian era, and in 1961 an inscription was dug up in Caesarea, from the period of the Roman occupation, actually naming the town of Nazareth.

124

We have already mentioned the question of how Jesus was crucified (see chapter four). When I was a student I was told that when a man was crucified by the Romans he was not nailed to a cross, but tied to it with ropes for the reasons already stated. Thus Thomas's request to put his finger into the nail marks was a fabrication, produced by people who had never seen a man crucified. The discovery in 1970 of the bones of a man who had been nailed to his cross is well documented (see A.E. Harvey, *Jesus and the Constraints of History* for both these examples).

These are two supposed errors in the Bible which I have seen explained in my lifetime, and there have been others. I am content to allow the scholars to continue their work on those problems that still remain.

The Bible is not only accurate, correct in what it asserts, but the text has remained basically unchanged down the centuries. In this way too it is *reliable*: it contains what authors, including people such as John and Paul and the rest, actually wrote down. Once we grasp just how ancient some parts of the Bible are (some parts of the Old Testament go back three thousand years), we realize that it is remarkable that the Bible has survived at all. But in fact we have some very old manuscripts to work from when we wish to check the text. There are more than five thousand manuscripts in Greek of the whole or some part of the New Testament.

Probably the most exciting discovery in the area of Bible documents was the discovery of the Dead Sea Scrolls. Scholars now tend to refer to them as the Qumran Scrolls, because we now know that they belonged to a community which lived in Qumran near the Dead Sea, not far from where the Scrolls were discovered. These scrolls consist mainly of Hebrew copies of the Old Testament books; in fact almost every book of the Old Testament is represented in the collection of scrolls. They were written somewhere around the time when Jesus lived in Palestine, much earlier than any Hebrew manuscripts we had previously had, and it was encouraging to see how they confirmed the belief that the text we had of the Old Testament was a reliable text.

Making use of all these manuscripts of both Old and New Testaments, scholars are continually at work to ensure that we have an accurate text to read. This is obviously very important to Christians since the Bible is almost the only source we have for any detailed knowledge about Jesus. Knowing that we have an accurate text is also important when we discuss our faith with others. Muslims, for example, explain the discrepancies between their Qur'an and the Christian Bible by insisting that the Bible is unreliable, that the Jews allowed their Old Testament to become corrupt, Christians allowed their New Testament to become corrupt, and the Qur'an is there to correct them both. But there is no evidence at all to support these accusations. None of the many ancient Bible manuscripts or early translations gives the story of Joseph as it appears in Sura 12, 'Joseph', and none of them gives the story of the birth of Jesus as it appears in Sura 19, 'Mary'. There are *legends* from which

Muhammad might have obtained his version of these stories, but there is no evidence anywhere that the Bible stories have been at all different from what we now have. The text of the Bible is reliable.

126   Incidentally, Muslims will sometimes say that the Qur'an is more reliable than the Bible because there are no variant manuscripts of the Qur'an, just one agreed Arabic text. What they say about the text of the Qur'an is true. But it is true only because when, some thirty years after the death of Muhammad, Zayd had finished the task given to him of putting together an accurate text of the Qur'an, all the variant manuscripts were destroyed!

Perhaps we should notice one more fact about the Bible: it is a *translated* book. The Old Testament was originally written in Hebrew and Aramaic, a later form of Hebrew; the New Testament was written in Greek (with a few words, the words actually spoken by Jesus, in Aramaic). Although Greek is still spoken today it is a very different kind of Greek from what we have in the New Testament. And although Hebrew has been revived and is the official language of the state of Israel that, too, is very different from the Hebrew of the Old Testament.

The world of the Old Testament and the world of New Testament times are very different from our own day; the customs were very different from our customs, so that it is not surprising that scholars sometimes have difficulty in translating Hebrew and Greek from centuries ago into the language of today. Fortunately there are many scholars, both Jews and Christians, studying the Bible, as well as archaeologists excavating sites named in the Bible, so that almost every day fresh light is being shed on the world of the Bible. As new translations of the Bible are produced so we find it more and more easy to understand the Bible's message.

It's also well to remember that many of these scholars and archaeologists are neither Christians nor Jews, but engage in their studies just out of a love for scholarship. Because they are always ready to check the work and the findings of others, we can be sure that what survives this close examination is honest, scholarly. Out of the labours of so many comes a Bible which is the authoritative, inspired, reliable word of God.

5. The contents of the Bible

The Bible is really a library in itself, and so it may be rather bewildering to the newcomer. There is no obvious order to it: the Psalms come in the middle for no apparent reason, and as soon as you get to the end of the history of the kings of Israel and Judah (1 & 2 Samuel, 1 & 2 Kings) the books of Chronicles start it all over again! And the world of the Bible is very different from ours, although today's world focuses almost as much attention on Jerusalem and what happens in Jerusalem as does the Bible.

Probably the best way to read the Bible is to use one of the schemes such as that produced by Scripture Union to take you through the Bible in five years.

But a summary of what's in the Bible may be helpful. The books of the Old Testament can be divided into four groups:

1. The five books of the law or the Pentateuch (referred to by Jews as the 'Torah'): Genesis, Exodus, Leviticus, Numbers, Deuteronomy
2. The 'Former Prophets' (to use the Jewish term) are, in fact, mainly historical: Joshua, Judges, Samuel, Kings.
3. The 'Writings' fall into three groups:
    Psalms, Proverbs, Job,
    The Song of Solomon (which is a beautiful love poem), Ruth, Lamentations, Ecclesiastes and Esther: these five are called 'The Five Scrolls',
    Daniel, Ezra-Nehemiah, Chronicles: again mainly historical
4. The 'Latter Prophets' include Isaiah, Jeremiah and Ezekiel, and also 'The Book of the Twelve': Hosea, Joel, Amos, Obadiah, Jonah, Micah, Nahum, Habakkuk, Zephaniah, Haggai, Zechariah, Malachi.

The New Testament books can be divided into three groups:

1. The Gospels, Matthew, Mark, Luke, John, with Acts, which was also most probably written by Luke.
2. The Letters: thirteen written by Paul, plus Hebrews, which some people still think was also written by Paul; and seven letters written by James, Peter, John and Jude.
3. Revelation, which is often compared to the last part of Daniel in the Old Testament, and is an account of how God will bring this world to its end, an apocalypse.

The Bible is a library well worth having, and its books are well worth reading. Some of the things it contains are difficult to understand, but much of it is very simple; exciting and challenging too. J.B. Phillips, who produced his own translation of the New Testament – originally for members of his church youth club – said that when he was working on the translation he repeatedly felt 'like an electrician re-wiring an ancient house without being able to turn the mains off'.

129

The particular power of the Bible is its ability to introduce us to Jesus.

An Overview of the Old and New Testaments.

Genesis
An account of beginnings: how it all began. The long history of Abraham, his children and grandchildren, explaining how they got to Palestine and then settled in Egypt.

⇐ **Noah**
⇐ **Abraham**
⇐ **The twelve sons of Jacob**
Reuben; Simeon; Levi; Judah; Issachar; Zebulun; Dan; Naphtali; Gad; Asher; Joseph; Benjamin

Exodus
How Moses took them out of Egypt, where they had become slaves, and led them back to the very borders of Palestine again.

⇐ **Moses**

Joshua
A new leader, Joshua, takes over. An account of the way the twelve tribes, descendants of Abraham, settled back into Palestine.

⇐ **Joshua**

Judges
An account of Joshua's successors, including Gideon and Samson, and how they repeatedly saved the nation from the surrounding peoples.

⇐ **The Judges**

1 Samuel
Samuel is sometimes called the last of the Judges and the first of the great prophets. A new start: Saul becomes the first king. The story of the growing conflict between Saul and David, and the death of Saul.

⇐ **Saul**
⇐ **David**

2 Samuel
David becomes king. His long reign.

1 Kings
David is succeeded by Solomon. Solomon builds the Temple in Jerusalem. Rebellion led by Jeroboam. The nation divided on Solomon's death, only two tribes, Judah and Levi, remaining faithful to Solomon's son Rehoboam. The prophet Elijah.

ISRAEL   JUDAH

2 Kings   Elisha succeeds Elijah. The succeeding kings of Israel, in the north, and Judah, in the south. Israel smashed, taken into exile. Judah struggles on, but they, too, go into exile, but to Babylon.

722BC

EXILE: THE TEN TRIBES ARE SCATTERED AND DISAPPEAR

⇐ **586BC** EXILE TO BABYLON
⇐ **537BC** THE RETURN FROM EXILE BEGINS

Ezra and Nehemiah   How the exiles from Babylon were allowed to return to Jerusalem, and how they rebuilt the city and the Temple.

⇐ **450BC** Ezra

⇐ Nehemiah

After Ezra and Nehemiah there is a gap of some 400 years in the historical record of the Bible. However there is a fascinating bridge between Old and New Testaments provided by the First Book of Maccabees, which records the events that affected Palestine after the death of Alexander the Great in 323BC. In particular it describes the great revolt under Judas Maccabaeus about 166BC. However 1 Maccabees is not one of the books of the Bible, but can be found in the Apocrypha.

⇐ **160BC** Judas Maccabaeus

Matthew, Mark, Luke, John   How John the Baptist, last of the great prophets, announced the coming of Jesus. Jesus' birth, life, teaching, death, resurrection.

⇐ **John the Baptist**
⇐ **JESUS-MESSIAH**

Acts   The acts of the first Christians, empowered by the Holy Spirit. How the Christian church began in Jerusalem and spread northwards into Syria. And how Paul took the good news throughout the Roman empire. Paul's arrest and imprisonment in Rome.

THE CHURCH

Revelation   A remarkable epilogue. John, exiled for his faith, is given a vision of the events of the end time.

8

Belonging Together

1. The church

That word 'church'! To many of us it suggests

- uncomfortable wooden pews (though many churches have found the courage to turf them out and replace them with more comfortable and more adaptable seating)
- long, tedious and largely irrelevant sermons (sometimes short but equally irrelevant)
- a strange language of thees and thous and thuses (now entirely removed from the New Revised Standard Version of the Bible and from most other modern translations).

The first church was very different. For one thing there were no special buildings for the Christians to meet in. They met in the homes of those Christians who were better off and lived in large enough houses to accommodate their local Christian communities. There was a church in Philemon's home (Philemon verse 2) and another in the home of a couple named Aquila and Priscilla (Romans 16:3–5). In fact the word 'church' in New Testament times never meant a building at all. The word referred to the Christian community in a village or some part of a city.

The New Testament notion of 'church' directs our attention to a significant feature of Christianity: Christians are not intended to go it alone. Becoming a Christian means becoming a member of a worldwide community, a family. The Head of the family is God. The family is now so large that we can no longer all meet together in one place. Indeed the early church grew so rapidly, three thousand in one day, that it soon had to do what we still do: it split up into smaller families.

133

The principle of togetherness is important for all of us. Right at the beginning God made clear a principle that is vital to every human being: it is not good to be alone (Genesis 2:18). Marriage was originally given to us not primarily for sex, but primarily so that we would not live alone, but in families. The church, similarly, is given to us not so that we should meet once or twice a week, on Sundays, to praise God and to worship, but so that we could be together as Christians. The church ensures that even if I am a child, and maybe my parents are not Christians, still I have a Christian family, the church. It means that even if I am married and my wife or husband is not a Christian, still I have a Christian family: the church. It means that the singles, the widows, the widowers, all have a Christian family to look to, to care for, in which they can find love and help.

Conversion means incorporation into the worldwide family, the church.

We need the church. We need the friendship of other Christians, their help when things go wrong, their encouragement when the way is hard. We need what the Bible calls *koinonia*, sharing. When my family returned from nineteen years as missionaries in Ethiopia we owned no furniture, no carpets, no curtains, nothing. We were going to live in a semi-detached house, with nothing in it. Nothing. One day a car drew up outside the little flat where we were living temporarily. A man from the church knocked at the door: 'Come and give me a hand.' I went outside. The car was loaded with curtain materials. 'And when you've decided on your curtains we'll go and choose your carpets.' A table and chairs from one family, a couple of beds from another, a refrigerator . . . and when we moved in the house was furnished. That's *koinonia*.

Jane has had a pretty rough life, and she really has no family. She worked for several years living in housing provided by her employer. Then came time to move on. She got a job. And the local council found her a flat. Unfurnished. But the church rallied round and again, *koinonia*. Her flat, *her* flat, was furnished.

The Christian life *is* something of a battle. Isn't all life? But there's an extra dimension for the Christian, there's the spiritual dimension, the spiritual battle. Those two king-' doms which we thought about in chapter two produce a kind of battlefield and we are caught up in the battle. Satan (no, not the comic figure in red tights and with horns and a pitchfork, but the real power behind the second kingdom) tests us just as once he tested Jesus. In fact just as he tested Job. The story of Job is helpful, here. Job was honest, upright, just, everything that God's people should be. He was also prosperous. Satan insisted that he was honest because he was prosperous. Satan removed the prosperity and he was still honest. Satan said that it was because he had his health. Satan took away his health . . . and at the end of the book of Job we find that Job is still honest. The same testings come to us: we lose our job, get behind with the mortgage, fall ill, and these things inevitably test our faith. The church is there to enable us to hold on.

♦ Christianity is not a Sunday afternoon stroll in the park. It is often a spiritual battle. Paul encourages us:

> *Put on the full armour of God so that you can take your stand against the devil's schemes. For our struggle is not against flesh and blood, but against the rulers, against the authorities, against the powers of this dark world and against the spiritual forces of evil in the heavenly realms.*
>
> (Ephesians 6:10–12)

If we are going to do that we need the encouragement of the church.

2. The two kingdoms

Jesus identified the two kingdoms for us, and he made clear the conflict that goes on between them. Jesus had healing powers, and he used those powers to heal a man who was blind and dumb. The question asked by the theologians of his day was: where did his healing power come from? They said that it came from 'Beel-zebul', the prince of the demons. But even their own theology agreed that this man's blindness and dumbness was caused by demonic power. So they were suggesting something quite absurd, that Jesus was using demonic power to destroy demonic power. Jesus said:

Every kingdom divided against itself is laid waste and no city or house divided against itself will stand;
and if Satan casts out Satan, he is divided against himself; how then will his kingdom stand?. . .
But if it is by the Spirit of God that I cast out demons, then the kingdom of God has come upon you.

So there they are: two kingdoms, the Kingdom of God and the Satanic kingdom, the Second Kingdom. And the action of Jesus makes it clear which of the two is the stronger. Now the Kingdom of God is one of the great themes of the New Testament. Jesus said that he had come to 'preach the good news of the Kingdom of God' (Luke 4:43). The Christian is in that kingdom, under the rule of the King. The Christian is also in the church. But the church is not the kingdom! Perhaps that's as well, since the church is often a great disappointment to us. We know what it should be like, but often it fails, it disappoints us.

Theologian John Macquarrie uses an unusual word to evoke a lovely picture: he calls the Kingdom of God 'the entelechy of the church'. The word 'entelechy' is most often used of flowers, where the flower is the 'entelechy' of the bud. The bud is not particularly attractive, but concealed inside it is all the beauty of the flower that will eventually appear. The church has potential. One day it will achieve that potential, when the kingdom bursts into sight.

The existence of the two kingdoms is a reminder of the Christian world-view: the recognition that behind the material there is the spiritual, behind what is seen there is the unseen, behind the 'you' that I can see there is another 'you', the real 'you', unseen, and very little understood by the rest of us. The two worlds are linked, intertwined in strange and sometimes unexpected ways. One of the great mysteries of science is the mystery of each person's self-awareness. I think about me. I even criticize my own actions. I am something more than a machine: I am a moral being, and that moral extra comes from the unseen, spiritual, world. The moral me has a conscience and, however careless, even defiant, I may become, that conscience is never quite extinguished. It is interesting that even in our prisons there is a 99.9 per cent agreement that some crimes put the criminal beyond the society even of criminals. Child molestation and child murder are just two of those crimes. And there are human emotions that are not material – love, hate, anger, joy, awe, hope, despair – and yet it is these emotions which actually determine the quality of life. Oddly enough it isn't bodily well-being that satisfies us; it is spiritual well-being. And by that I don't just mean religion; I mean the experience, the feeling, of love and joy and hope on the one side or the feeling of rage, hatred, despair on the other.

Christians can't be materialists. Out of our faith we actually have a 'science', a 'theology', a 'philosophy', a world-view which we can explain, that enables us to live our lives in a meaningful way.

The Christian life is often a life of conflict, conflict with that Second Kingdom. Jesus experienced the same conflict. Before he began his teaching and healing work Jesus withdrew to the desert and there he was tested, tempted. (There is nothing sinful about experiencing temptation. As Martin Luther is alleged to have said, speaking about temptations, 'You can't stop the birds from flying over your head, but you can stop them building their nests in your hair'!)

There must have been many other occasions when Jesus was tempted, since during his lifetime he was tempted by all the things that tempt us (Hebrews 4:15). He didn't give in to temptation and we do. To help us to stand against temptation we need the help of the church, and we need the strength of the Holy Spirit. That's just one of the reasons why the church should be more than a Sunday congregation: I need the help and encouragement of the church family on Monday too!

So the church is the bud out of which the Kingdom of God will come . . . the place where I find my family so that I am not alone . . . where I can find strength when I am tempted . . . where I can be corrected when I go wrong. Another great theologian described the church as that body of people from within which alone it is possible to know the world as it is. I recall listening in amazement to the BBC reporting the progress of the Six Days War in July 1967. As the Israelis captured Jerusalem, the Golan Heights, the Gaza Strip, and on down south as far as the Suez Canal, I listened and found myself waiting for some commentator to mention the religious dimension as well as the military dimension. But none of them ever did. From inside the church I could see an extra dimension of understanding denied to them. It was not that I necessarily approved of all that the Israelis did, simply because they were Jewish — but still I could see more in that conflict than even the best of the BBC's professional commentators.

The divided church

The church is divided. There are thousands of different groups, denominations, divided on all sorts of issues, some of them important, some of them trivial. But as Ephesians 4:4 puts it, there is just one Body: you are either part of it or you are outside of it.

The division of the churches is bad, because it confuses people outside who are trying to get in. On which door should they knock? It is bad because we do not simply accept the divisions: we fight with one another, disagree, criticize – even go to court to decide which of two parties can use a building for their worship.

But there is a positive side to these divisions. They bring variety to the church. Some people like a 'pop music' approach to worship and they can find a pop music type of church. Some people like a grand opera approach to worship and they can find an opera-style church. The trouble comes when the pop worshippers insist that everybody must have pop music services, or the opera churches suggest that theirs is the only true worship.

Actually most Christians don't really know why they are in the sort of church they belong to. Often they're there because their parents were, or because the church is not too far from home, or because their friends go there. Few Methodists know why they aren't Baptists and few Baptists know why they aren't United Reformed.

Some years ago I wrote an article in the *British Weekly*, suggesting this, and a couple of weeks later an irate member of the Plymouth Brethren wrote in to say that he most certainly did know why he wasn't Baptist. He gave ten reasons. The editor published his letter . . . but in fact every one of his ten reasons showed that he simply didn't know what Baptists do and believe.

140

Of course Christians are sometimes in genuine disagreement about Christian beliefs. But many of our differences are not, in fact, doctrinal at all. And differences do serve the purpose of the Second Kingdom. C.S. Lewis makes this point sharply but amusingly. His *Screwtape Letters* contains letters written by Screwtape, a rather superior tempter, under-Secretary to a Department, to Wormwood, a junior tempter. He advises Wormwood how to deal with a new Christian seeking to join a church:

> I think I warned you before that if your patient can't be kept out of the church, he ought at least to be violently attached to some party within it. I don't mean on really important doctrinal issues: about those, the more lukewarm he is the better. And it isn't the doctrines on which we chiefly depend for producing malice. The real fun is working up hatred between those who say 'mass' and those who say 'holy communion', when neither party could possibly state the difference between, say, Hooker's doctrine and Thomas Aquinas' in any form which would hold water for five minutes.
>
> (*Screwtape Letters*, chapter 16)

Christians have good reason to be ashamed of the divisions within the church. It was Jesus himself who prayed for the unity of the church:

> *My prayer is not for them (the apostles) alone. I pray also for those who will believe in me through their message, that all of them may be one, Father, just as you are in me and I am in you. May they also be in us, so that the world may believe that you have sent me. I have given them the glory that*

you gave me, that they may be one as we are one: I in them and you in me.
May they be brought to complete unity to let the world know that you sent
me and have loved them even as you have loved me.

(John 17:20–23)

This prayer of Jesus is interesting, because it indicates the kind of unity that he has in mind for his church: it is like the unity that there is between the Father and the Son. This does not suggest *integration*, as though the Son ceased to be the Son, and lost his identity. The unity between Father and Son is one of will and purpose and love. And that is the kind of unity we should look for amongst the churches.

This is just one of the reasons why I feel that the World Council of Churches has got it wrong. The Council has done its best to promote schemes of integration in which real differences are submerged and churches lose their identity. Rather we should be looking for unity of purpose, accepting the genuine differences of opinion that exist amongst us. The following sums it up very clearly:

Be completely humble and gentle, be patient, bearing with one another in
love. Make every effort to keep the unity of the Spirit through the bond of
peace. There is one body and one Spirit – just as you were called to one hope
when you were called – one Lord, one faith, one baptism, one God and
Father of all, who is over all, and through all and in all.

But to each one of us grace has been given, as Christ apportioned it . . .
It was he who gave some to be apostles, some prophets, some to be evangelists
and some to be pastors and teachers, to prepare God's people for works of
service, so that the body of Christ may be built up until we all reach unity
in the faith and in the knowledge of the Son of God, and become mature,
attaining to the whole measure of the fullness of Christ.

Then we will no longer be infants, tossed back and forth by the waves,
and blown here and there by every wind of teaching and by the cunning and

craftiness of men in their deceitful scheming. Instead, speaking the truth in love, we will in all things grow up into him who is the Head, that is Christ. From him the whole body, joined and held together by every supporting ligament, grows and builds itself up in love, as each part does its work.

(Ephesians 4:2–7; 11–16)

142

4. But what is the church *for*?

The church is there primarily for three things: worship, witness, community.

(i) The church is there for worship

Of course it is possible to worship God on your own, but it is a marvellous thing to be able to join together with other Christians, maybe hundreds of them, to worship God as a family. Jesus taught his followers only one prayer, and that prayer began '*Our* Father' (Matthew 6:9–13). You can't pray that prayer on your own; it's a family prayer.

Christians are expected to meet together regularly to worship God. God is at the heart of the Christian understanding of worship. Worship is the appropriate response to an awareness of the presence of God. That response may be a sense of awe and wonder, a sense of joy, a sense of deep sadness (maybe because that presence brings with it a sense of our own sin) or it may be activity: there is something to be done now that God has come to me. This awareness of the presence of God can't be manufactured. It comes to us in unexpected ways: a particular hymn, a piece of poetry, a reading from the Bible, a miraculous healing, a conversion. Suddenly we are aware, as Jacob was (Genesis 28:17), that 'God is in this place, and I did not know it.' Jacob reacted with awe, but that is not the only possible response.

Jacob was alone when he had that experience, but we often find the experience when we are with others, and the reason for that is clear. Jesus once took a well-known saying of the rabbis – 'Where two or three are gathered to study the Torah (the Law of Moses) there God is with them' – and re-phrased it: 'Where two or three are gathered together in my name, there am I with them' (Matthew 18:20). If Jesus is somehow with us when we meet together it ought not to be difficult to become aware of his presence . . . and to worship.

(ii) The church is there for witness

Christians are people who have encountered God through Jesus. Christians are not people who pretend to be better than everyone else, but people who are humble enough to admit their sins, their bad temper, their selfishness, to ask forgiveness, and to receive it as his free gift. They are people who enjoy that wonderful sense of lightness that comes from knowing that the past is forgiven. Not unnaturally Christians are people who want to share that experience with others.

And there's more to it than that. Christians are also people who have received a new strength, through the Holy Spirit, strength to do better, strength to abandon old vices, strength to put on new virtues. More even than that, Christians are people who have a new way of looking at the world, a new way of understanding a world that is otherwise inexplicable.

Undoubtedly there are people who are outside the church, outside all religion, who are questioning the meaning of life, trying to make sense of the world, and who understandably want to ask of any suggested solution, 'But does it *work*?' The Christian is able to reply: 'Yes, Christianity *does* work, because it works for me.' We may not be able to explain *how* it works: who knows how it is that Christ's death and resurrection deals with our sin? But we can know that it does work.

We see this in the story about the blind man in John 9. After Jesus had restored his sight, the Pharisees interrogated the man about this miracle. Then they started a discussion about the theology of healing: 'We know that this man [Jesus] is a sinner'. He couldn't have the power to heal. The man who had been healed was no theologian and couldn't comment on that. But he stuck firmly to what he knew:

> *Whether he is a sinner or not, I don't know.*
> *One thing I do know: I was blind but now I see!*

> (John 11: 25)

We may not have experienced anything quite as dramatic as that, but surely God has been at work in our lives, somewhere, and we can tell others about *that*.

Again, we may not be able to talk about what God has done for us, but certainly the kind of lives that we live should illustrate his work in us? Christians should be excellent neighbours, good employers and employees, excellent wives, husbands, sons, daughters, mothers, fathers. Christianity is intended to produce better people, and those outside the church are impressed far more by good people than they are by great sermons. And yet inevitably the time will come when we will be asked about our faith. I remember an occasion when a man was taken into hospital in Addis Ababa, suffering from schizophrenia. His wife was desperate. She knew nobody and yet her husband needed more help than the understaffed hospital could give. We did our best to help. We took hot meals into the hospital for her. We took turns watching over her husband while she went off to get some rest. We carried on like this for maybe a month, and I suppose that all that time she was watching us, trying to see what our motives might be. One day we were standing on the balcony outside her husband's room, and suddenly she turned to me and asked, 'Peter, how can I become a Christian?'

We need to be able to answer a question like that, to give some kind of explanation of why we are what we are.

There's overseas witness, too, witness to the wider world. Jesus commanded his first followers to go into the whole world, to make more Christians, to teach them how to follow him. We need to follow their example, to go. But we also have to receive witnesses from other countries more Christian than we are, as they come to tell us what God has done in them. The marvellous fact is that in the whole world God is at work, in his church, through his church, helping Christians to grow up, helping those who aren't Christians to join the family.

(iii) The church is for community

'Community' has two aspects to it, the church's relationship to other Christians and the church's relationship to the non-Christian world.

The New Testament word for fellowship, community, is *koinonia*, sharing. In the New Testament and in life today, this is the obvious characteristic of the church as a family. This 'family' idea often astonishes people who aren't Christians. During the two years I spent in the Royal Air Force, I was sent to the north of England. The first Sunday I was permitted to leave the base I set off to find a church. Late that night I returned to camp. Then the questions began: Where had I spent the day? I went to church. That was clear enough. But then, where did I have my dinner? Oh, some people invited me to their home for dinner. Did I know them? No, we'd never met before. Well, what about tea? Oh, another family asked me to tea. And church again in the evening, I suppose? Right. And then someone else took me home for supper . . . and, no, I didn't know any of them previously. The other men couldn't understand this Christian family idea.

This notion of sharing is clearly demonstrated in the life of the first Christians. On the Day of Pentecost, about six weeks after the crucifixion, Peter preached to a great crowd of Jews, and some three thousand responded. What did they do?

> *They devoted themselves to the apostles' teaching, and to the fellowship, to the breaking of bread and to prayer . . . . All the believers were together and had everything in common . . . . They broke bread in their homes and ate together with glad and sincere hearts, praising God and enjoying the favour of all the people*

(Acts 2:42–47)

But the church is involved in another kind of relationship – the relationship with the rest of society, with people who are not Christians. This can't really be called *koinonia*, because there may be very little in common for them all to share. The church offers *philanthropia*, friendship, caring. The church does not treat its non-Christian neighbours as enemies. It is always there, reaching out in friendship, ready to help.

Paul wrote to the Christians in Galatia: '*Therefore, as we have opportunity let us do good to all people*' (Galatians 6:10). This means that the local church should be offering uncon-ditional love to everyone, perhaps especially to those who are left unloved by others. The fact that Christians behave like this helps to explain the comparatively large numbers of 'odd' people we find in the churches: they are often people who are left out by the rest of society.

At the international level we find again that Christians reach out to others just out of compassion. Organizations such as Tear Fund and Christian Aid take the gifts of Christians from this country and use the money, millions of pounds each year, to help the hungry, the homeless, the sick, in every part of the world. The church is *not* isolated from the real world; it is deeply involved in its every pain.

I was in Ethiopia during the famine years. With the help of Tear Fund we took a lorry load of grain up north into the famine area. We halted in a huge Muslim market area in order to transfer our sacks of grain onto mules for the next part of the journey. The market place was thronged with Muslims, and some of them gathered round our truck. I talked with them – they were startled to find that I spoke their language. They began to call out to the others that here was a *ferenj*, a foreigner, who spoke their language!

They surrounded the truck. And they demanded that I explain why we were there bringing grain to their people. 'We know that you are Christians. You know that we are Muslims. But you don't ask those starving people up there whether they are Muslims or Christians; you just feed them. There are Muslims back in Addis Ababa, but they haven't come to feed us. So why do you?'

148

Help like this is not bait to hook converts. It is simply doing what Jesus would want us to do – to express fellowship with all humanity.

9

The Goal of History

If history goes on for ever – that's boring. If history simply
fades away – that's anticlimax. If history goes round and
round in circles life is pointless. But the Bible promises
something different: it says history is heading towards a
grand climax.

1. The Christian world-view

We started this book by asking some basic questions. Each
of the world's religions offers answers which indicate their
individual world-view. Accepting a religion means accepting the world-view of that religion. There are as many
world-views as there are religions, and they are all different.
The Christian world-view can be set out clearly and
concisely.

The world is not a mere cosmic accident. Whether we
take a big bang theory of the origin of the universe or prefer
some other scientific explanation of the 'how', the Bible
insists on a 'who': God created it.

Humankind is not merely the chance product of evolution, one cosmic accident among many. We are different
from all other forms of life because we share in the nature
of God, we were created in the image of God (Genesis

1:26). God has planted within us the concept of eternity, so that we know there is something beyond time.

Life is unsatisfactory. Between the two apparent boundaries of birth and death life does not seem to make sense. But it is unsatisfactory not merely as a result of our ignorance, but as a result of our sin. It is useless to try to live a meaningful life apart from God

The unsatisfactoriness of life will never be resolved by human invention or human wisdom, by human governments or by international organizations, however well-meaning they may be. The only answer to our problems is reconciliation with God. Only in this way can we be reconciled to each other.

We can be reconciled to God through Christ. The greatest event in human history was not that man stood on the moon, but that God stood on the earth, was 'lifted up' on a cross, died, and rose from that death.

Reconciliation with God is accompanied by the gift of the Holy Spirit, who enables us to live out the new life that Christ gives. On the one hand he enables us to defeat sin, and on the other hand he empowers us to live the kind of lives we have always known we should live.

God does not call us to mere individualism, but throughout the world he calls his people into communities, churches. Through these churches Christians witness to the world and share with the world. They represent on earth the practical outworking of the compassion of God.

But the church also has to bring a warning, that the Kingdom of God, the rule of God, is a reality standing over against the Second Kingdom. Every person must be in the one kingdom or in the other.

The world will not merely run down as energy becomes less and less available (as science has suggested), nor will it end in some terrifying but unintended catastrophic explosion. It will end through a definite act of God.

The end of the world's history will usher in judgment, and it is this judgment that will finally balance the books and establish God's justice. Each of us will have to give account of ourselves to a God who knows not only what we have done, but also what we could have done; not only our actions, but the motives that prompted those actions.

2. The idea of judgment

The New Testament speaks repeatedly of a last judgment, a judgment where we are all required to give an account of ourselves (Romans 14:12). The judgment will be based on:

♦ Our own responsibility for our own decisions –
♦ God's perfect knowledge of us: our acts and our motives –
♦ Our knowledge of God –
♦ Our relationship to Christ.

We are responsible for our lives. That is part of being human, part of adult responsibility. Children may blame their parents for their problems, but adults must take responsibility for their own lives. But often we don't understand the reasons for our own actions. We may see someone writing a generous cheque for a missionary society, but we don't know *why* the cheque is being written. Is it to be able to boast of giving generously or is it from a concern for those to whom the mission ministers? Is it an attempt to compensate for some sin, an attempt to buy God off? A poor person steals a loaf of bread. Is it simply that the family has nothing to eat? Is it because they have all got accustomed to living by stealing? We don't know. God does. Our judgment will be based on God's knowledge of us, as well as of our actions.

For us to attempt to assess someone's moral standing is like an accountant attempting to produce a statement of a large firm's financial situation while being allowed access to just one cheque book in ten, one computer record out of fifty, one financial statement from a decade. Without the full facts the task is impossible. And yet how quick we are to judge one another!

Paul begins his letter to the church at Rome with a carefully argued summary of why it is that we are all of us – the Jews who have had God's Law, the Gentiles who had no such revelation – in the same boat, all failures, all facing judgment. One day, he says, all of our secrets will be exposed:

> *This will take place on the day when God will judge men's secrets through Jesus Christ, as my gospel declares.*
>
> (Romans 2:16)

It is surely significant that Paul relates this judgment to Christ. This suggests that the last judgment is not a mere adding up of good deeds, to be credited against our bad deeds to yield either a credit or a debit balance. It is

THE GOAL OF HISTORY

essentially a judgment which relates to our relationship to Jesus. Jesus, God incarnate, came for us, died for us, rose again from the dead for us. So how have we responded?

> *But now he has appeared once, for all, at the end of the ages, to do away with sin by the sacrifice of himself. Just as man is destined to die once, and after that to face judgment, so Christ was sacrificed once to take away the sins of many people, and he will appear a second time, not to bear sin, but to bring salvation to those who are waiting for him.*
>
> (Hebrews 9:26–28)

At this point we have begun to put together an outline of the Bible's teaching on the day of judgment. Jesus is to come again, 'he will appear a second time'. This fact was announced to Jesus' followers immediately after the ascension. Jesus had left them, 'gone up' to be concealed from them by clouds (perhaps the *shekinah* glory-clouds, mentioned in Old Testament passages such as Exodus 40:34–35 and in the story of the transfiguration in Luke 9:18–36). While they were still standing there they were told:

> *This same Jesus, who has been taken from you into heaven, will come back in the same way you have seen him go into heaven.*
>
> (Acts 1:11)

The actual return is vividly pictured in 1 Thessalonians 4:16:

> *For the Lord himself will come down from heaven with a loud command, with the voice of the archangel, and with the trumpet call of God.*

and Paul adds a further detail to the picture:

> *. . . we will all be changed – in a flash, in the twinkling of an eye, at the last trumpet. For the trumpet will sound, the dead will be raised imperishable, and we will be changed.*
>
> (1 Corinthians 15:51–52)

Jesus himself added a striking illustration of the suddenness of the end:

> *Two men will be in the field; one will be taken and the other left. Two women will be grinding with a hand mill; one will be taken and the other left.*

(Matthew 24:40–41)

We are left to imagine the astonishment of the man left alone in the field, or the woman whose friend has simply vanished.

Often critics have smiled at what they consider the naive and fanciful ideas of Christianity concerning the end time. There's nothing particularly modern about this tendency. Almost two thousand years ago Peter knew people who were asking:

> *Where is this 'coming' he promised? Ever since our fathers died everything goes on as it has since the beginning of creation.*

(2 Peter 3:4)

In fact, as Peter comments drily, things *haven't* gone on smoothly from one generation to the next. Great upheavals have occurred in the world: flood, famine, earthquake. Empires have come and gone, nations have risen to prominence only to disappear from the world scene. New inventions have come radically to change our lives. Life is the experience of change. God sees not merely the change but also the ultimate transformation. Isaiah points to God's activity in the world:

> *I foretold things long ago,*
> *my mouth announced them and I made them known;*
> *then suddenly I acted, and they came to pass.*

(Isaiah 48:3)

There is to be a day of judgment, and that judgment will demonstrate God's perfect justice:

> *For he has set a day when he will judge the world with justice by the man he has appointed. He has given proof of this to all men by raising him from the dead.*

(Acts 17:31)   155

This raises a problem. What about the fate of the vast majority of humankind throughout history? Of all those who have ever lived, perhaps 99 per cent have never heard the Good News. How are they to be judged 'with justice'? It used to be widely believed that only those who had somehow 'received Christ as their personal Saviour' could be saved. But this is obviously wrong:

- the people of the Old Testament did not know about Jesus, and yet Abraham and Isaac and Jacob are already safe home in the Kingdom (Luke 13:28).
- babies and little children who die before they can know about Jesus, much less 'receive him as Saviour', are also taken by all of us to be safe in heaven.
- those who because of mental illness may be quite unable to understand the Good News, even if they heard it, are surely not eternally lost simply because of their illness? They too find the mercy of God.

And the rest? The vast majority who have never heard of Jesus? Well, the Bible reminds us that God has revealed himself in at least three ways – through the prophets, through Jesus (Hebrews 1:1–2), and through creation where his invisible nature, his eternal power, his deity, are clearly shown (Romans 1:20). The Bible says that God created the world in such a way that we *could* find him through it. When Paul visited Athens he told the people there:

> *God made from one every nation of men to live on all the face of the earth, having determined allotted periods and the boundaries of their habitations, that they should seek God, in the hope that they might feel after him and find him.*

(Acts 17:26–27)

It seems that people who, through no fault of their own (in fact through *our* fault!) have never heard the Good News about Jesus might be able to find God through the world he made.

It's worth pointing out that this problem of the fate of those who have never heard about Jesus is not my problem and it's not your problem. We *have* heard. The problem for us is our response to what we have heard. If you have read through this book and reached this point then you know enough to make a decision about you and Jesus. Is he to be your Saviour? This really is important.

We started this book by talking about the fundamental questions we all ask about the meaning of life and the unfairness of life. I have tried to show you the Christian answers to these questions. Yes, life *is* unfair, and it *is* full of suffering. This is because ours is a fallen world, a world overflowing with a multitude of individual falls, personal acts of disobedience – sins. Yet God stepped into this world, deliberately choosing to be poor, accepting betrayal, a mockery of a trial, a cruel death, to bear away our sins. Christ conquered death, rose from the grave, was seen by his followers, ascended back to heaven, sent his Spirit to be in us and to enable us to live the kind of lives we ought to live. But what if we choose to shrug our shoulders and walk away from all this? In their case –

If we deliberately keep on sinning after we have received the knowledge of the truth, no sacrifice for sins is left, but only a fearful expectation of judgment.
(Hebrews 10:26)

But can we escape from that great judgment? We certainly can! John's dramatic vision of the judgment (Revelation 20:11–21:4) contains a reference to two books. In one the acts of all humankind are recorded. The other is described as the 'Book of Life'. It's referred to again in Revelation 21:27, but with a significant addition: here it is called 'the Lamb's Book of Life'. It may seem an odd title for a book. But if you know your Bible well enough it will probably remind you at once of the beginning of John's gospel, where John-the-Baptizer sees Jesus and calls out to the crowd around him:

Look, the Lamb of God who takes away the sin of the world!

The Lamb's Book of Life? The Lamb who takes away the sin of the world? Who or what is this 'Lamb'?

♦ The word may refer to Isaiah 53:7, where the Servant of the Lord is is being described and Isaiah says that he was 'led like a lamb to the slaughter'. So Jesus was that Servant, and when he was crucified he was fulfilling this prophecy.

♦ It almost certainly refers to something that happened during that most important of all events in Jewish history, the Exodus, when each family, enslaved in Egypt, sacrificed a lamb as a substitute for the firstborn of the family

(Exodus 12:21). In memory of that occasion a lamb was sacrificed in the Temple in Jerusalem every morning and every evening, even in Jesus' time.

The people listening to John-the-Baptizer would not have needed this explanation when they first heard John's words. And the people reading the book of Revelation, too, would have needed no explanation: the Lamb had died as their sacrifice, as their substitute, and those who followed the Lamb would have their names written down in the Lamb's book. The imagery sounds odd to us, but the message is clear – those who are followers of Jesus have their names written down in the Book of Life, and it is they who enter heaven (Revelation 21:27).

What about hell? That is a reality, too. We no more know what it is like than we know what heaven is like. Heaven is certainly not literally a gigantic golden cube, as it is described in Revelation 21:16. And hell is not a vast flaming pit, although this is how the Bible describes it. Hell is the destiny of those who have deliberately rejected the claims of Jesus. Such people may not enter heaven. But what exactly hell is we don't know. The illustration of fire is repeatedly used of hell. Now fire can do two things: it can burn and so cause pain, or it can burn and so destroy. Some people believe that the 'fire' of hell is a fire that destroys. After all, death and Hades are thrown into the Lake of Fire, and it doesn't make sense to talk of death and Hades suffering; they are to be destroyed. Those who are 'cast into the Lake of Fire' are similarly destroyed. This idea is referred to as conditional immortality: only some people, the saved, become immortal.

Others believe that the suffering caused by the flames of hell does go on for ever. They point out that the same Greek word – *aiônios*, 'eternal' – is used for the eternal punishment and for the eternal life.

For myself I have a further problem. If time was created at the same moment as the universe was created, and it seems that it was, then to think either of eternal life or of hell as 'going on and on for ever' is a mistake. There is no yesterday and no tomorrow in heaven, or in hell, for that matter. But then I can't imagine an unending 'now' and neither can anyone else!

What we must take seriously is the warning about the alternative to eternal life. It is eternal 'unlife'.

3. The idea of heaven

Heaven is the realization of a creation purpose. What God intended in Genesis 1 becomes fact in Revelation 22. Through all the long conflict between the two kingdoms the eternal reality has never changed: the Second Kingdom has power, but it has no power ultimately to defy God's will. At creation time was created. At the end of the world time comes to an end, the great judgment of us all takes place, and the new redeemed worshipping community enters heaven. But what is the Christian heaven like?

♦ **Heaven is a place of celebration, a wedding feast, a banquet** (Revelation 19:9):

Then the angel said to me, 'Write: "Blessed are those who are invited to the wedding supper of the Lamb!"'

Through the centuries this is how Jewish thought has always pictured the coming kingdom; as a place of solemnity, yes, but above all a place of celebration, a great celestial party. I have a personal problem about this that I share with C.S. Lewis. I don't like parties. I recall with deep understanding, sympathy and amusement how C.S. Lewis reacted when other boys invited him to their birthday parties: 'What harm had I ever done to them? I had never invited them to my parties'! But this wedding banquet will be different. Even people like C.S. Lewis – and me – will be able to enjoy this party!

♦ **Heaven marks the end of human pain** (Revelation 21:3–4):

I heard a loud voice from the throne saying, 'Now the dwelling of God is with men, and he will live with them. They will be his people, and God himself will be with them and be their God. He will wipe away every tear from their eyes. There will be no more death or mourning or crying or pain, for the old order of things has passed away.'

I think back over the years and the numerous times when I have read these words at a funeral service. How I have yearned for that day to come, to see an end of the tears, the pain. Well, it will come.

♦ **In heaven there is no night, only pure glorious, brilliant light** (Revelation 21:22–24):

I did not see a temple in the city, because the Lord God Almighty and the Lamb are its temple. The city does not need the sun or the moon to shine on it, for the glory of God gives it light, and the Lamb is its lamp. The nations will walk by its light . . . .

I recall preaching one Sunday, in the open air, way down in the south of Ethiopia. Thousands had gathered for the service. I preached (as I was expected to do) for maybe ninety minutes. Then I stepped off the rough platform and walked towards where my mule was tethered. An elder called after me. Where did I think I was going? Home, of course. It was a long journey, and if I didn't start now it would be dark before I got there. And I had no lantern, no torch, with me. 'You can't go yet. We're going to have another service. You must preach again. We'll provide you with a guide and a torch.' I agreed, preached again, another ninety minutes. Then, at last, we set off, my guide alongside me, carrying the torch. As it grew dusk I saw him shaking the torch. It wouldn't work. I investigated. No batteries! Night fell suddenly, as it is does in Africa, and still we had miles to go. The hyenas were soon around us. The track was scarcely visible. We felt rather than saw the way ahead. Some four hours later I reached home. I fell into a chair and rested a few minutes, then made to get up to ensure that my guide had a meal and a bed. But I couldn't get up: my muscles simply cramped up, complaining bitterly about four hours of tense walking in the dark.

And that's a good picture of what we are all doing now. We are walking in the dark, the way ahead unclear, walking on by faith and not by sight. But there is heaven ahead where there are no dark paths, no uncertainties, only glorious light.

♦ **Heaven is free of all that is evil.** There will be no smut, no crudity (Revelation 21:25–27):

> *Nothing impure will ever enter it, nor will anyone who does what is shameful or deceitful, but only those whose names are written in the Lamb's book of life.*

Here we live in the real but fallen world, a dark world, a dirty world. We watch the television set, our fingers ready to switch off when the inevitable smut comes. You've seen it, as I have. The jolly comedian who specializes in blue jokes and racism. The famed comedienne with a knowing smirk on her face as she shares a particularly crude bit of smut – 'You see, women can be just as dirty as you men!' Well, none of that in heaven.

◆ **Heaven is Eden restored.** The beginning and end of our Bible are brought together (Genesis 2:8–10):

> *Now the Lord God had planted a garden in the east, in Eden; and there he put the man he had formed. And the Lord God made all kinds of trees grow out of the ground – trees that were pleasing to the eye and good for food. In the middle of the garden were the tree of life and the tree of the knowledge of good and evil. A river watering the garden flowed from Eden.*

The garden appears again in Revelation 22:1–2, but without the tree of the knowledge of good and evil:

> *Then the angel showed me the river of the water of life, as clear as crystal, flowing from the throne of God and of the Lamb down the middle of the great street of the city. On each side of the river stood the tree of life, bearing twelve crops of fruit, yielding its fruit every month.*

The tree of life now becomes trees bearing abundant fruit, the waters of the great river are now clear and life-giving.

162

♦ **God himself is the focus of heaven** (Revelation 22:1–5):

The throne of God and of the Lamb will be in the city, and his servants will serve him. They will see his face, and his name will be on their foreheads. There will be no more night. They will not need the light of a lamp or the light of the sun, for the Lord God will give them light. And they will reign for ever and ever.

What a point at which to end! This is the Christian story: of a world created by God, spoiled by humanity, redeemed in sheer grace by a Saviour, moving towards a sure destination, the culmination of all history when justice triumphs at last, and a heaven is revealed where the Triune God reigns in glory amidst a perfected worshipping community.

This is the vision that underlies Michael Saward's hymn:

Lord of the cross of shame, set my cold heart aflame
With love for you, my Saviour and my Master.
Who on that lonely day bore all my sin away,
And saved me from the judgment and disaster.

Lord of my life today, teach me to live and pray
As one who knows the joy of sins forgiven.
So may I ever be, now and eternally,
One with my fellow-citizens in heaven.